LONDON BY BUS

CD
BUS STOP
Crouch End Broadway
towards Alexandra Park
or Archway
W5
W7
Buy tickets before
boarding on route W7
safehouse
THE
SAFEHOUSE
99p
DEAL
Need storage?
You won't find
cheaper!
555 WHITE HART LANE
0800 597 5000
www.safehouse-ss.com
Waitrose
FREE
Home
Delivery!
Lower
Prices +
Great
Offers
2 FOR
£2
ALL
£4.75
EACH

introduction

Going by bus is not the quickest way to travel around London. If you want to get from A to B with time to spare, then – like millions of commuters each weekday morning – take the tube. If, however, you want to see more of the capital than just the walls of a sooty tunnel and your fellow passengers' armpits, climb aboard one of the city's iconic red double-deckers. The London bus made its first appearance on the city streets back in 1829 – when it was pulled between Paddington Station and the City by horses – and as the capital has expanded, so too has the bus network. You can now travel from one end of the city to another without ever having to go underground.

The idea for **London By Bus** came to me when I moved to the capital 15 years ago. After a day of looking for flatshares, I jumped on the first bus that displayed the name of somewhere I recognised and took my seat on the top deck. Having only previously visited London as a tourist, I was amazed this most functional type of public transport took me past the Houses of Parliament, Trafalgar Square, Piccadilly Circus, Chinatown – all the landmarks that had been on my sightseeing wish list as a wide-eyed daytripper from Sheffield. I remember passing people queuing for an open-top bus, and wondering why they didn't just buy a cheap travelcard and see everything at their own pace.

This book allows you to do just that. Not only will you visit the city's main sights but also, on these quirky 25 themed journeys, you will be taken into fascinating, hidden corners of the capital that are well off the beaten track. **London By Bus** is as much for Londoners who only know the bus route that takes them to work as it is for those who are visiting for the first time. It's about seeing the city differently and experiencing it in the most authentic way possible. The capital's double-deckers cut across all social divides, and you'll be sharing carriage space with those who use them every day – from the Orthodox Jews of Stamford Hill and Punjabi-speakers of Southall to wealthy City traders and Notting Hill trustafarians.

So, choose your themed journey from the following pages, download the route details to your Smartphone and pick up a one-day travelcard from any newsagent or tube station. You're ready to experience the real London.

Rufus Purdy, Crouch End, London, July 2012

contents

116

132

Buff
Bronze
Bare
172

how to use this book

First, buy a travelcard...

As each of the journeys in this book involve several buses, the most economical way to travel is to purchase a one-day **Zone 1-4 travelcard**, which allows you unlimited travel within central London and the outlying districts featured in this book. Alternatively, buy an **Oyster Card**, which you can use as a digital one-day pass. Both are availabl from tube stations; while most newsagents sell them, too. At the time of writing, a one-da pass costs £7.70 for off-peak use (any time after 9.30am) and £10.60 for unrestricte travel. If you're planning to do several of the themed journeys in **London By Bus**, it's worth getting a seven-day Zone 1-4 travelcard, which currently costs £41.80.

Then download the journey to your Smartphone...

Each of the **QR-codes** in this book – the crossword-like squares that appear on the maps that accompany each journey – provides access to a website from which you ca download jpeg or pdf versions of each route. This allows you to store all the details o an iPhone or other Smartphone, and have them to hand, rather than having to carry the book around with you. Downloading the information to your phone is simple...

Most Smartphones come with a QR-code reader. If you don't have a QR-code reade on your Smartphone, go to your App store to download one. We recommend i-nigm

Once you've downloaded the QR-code reader, launch it as you would any other Ap Your phone's camera will automatically start looking for a QR-code to scan, so line i up over the one that accompanies the journey you want to prepare.

Your phone will then scan the QR-code and take you directly to the webpage. Click either the pdf or jpeg file, and it will be downloaded to your Photo Gallery or Downloads folder. You will then be able to access and enlarge these files at any tim

iPhone users should select the jpeg option. Once the file has opened, simply tap you screen and you will be able to save it to the Camera Roll in your Photos folder.

Finally, once you're at the bus stop...

As some buses do not travel the full length of their designated routes (though this rarely affects travel within central London), we felt it would be confusing to identify the bus you need by its supposed final destination. All routes in this book go in two directions, so to differentiate them we've stated the direction of travel – northbound, westbound, etc – as well as the name of the stops you need to get on and off at. If you are confused about which direction the bus is going in, either refer to the map attached to each bus stop or ask the driver if he's going to the destination you're headed for.

lease note that, unless clearly specified otherwise, the names of the stops (in bold ype in the journey details) you require to complete each journey are always bus tops. When 'Euston Station' is stated, for example, this refers to a specific bus stop ather than the rail terminus nearby. Almost all London buses announce the name of he stop they are approaching, and most clearly display this information on an LED creen at the front of each deck. If you pay attention to these, you'll have no problem egotiating the 25 themed journeys in this book.

Vhen you board the bus, either show the driver your travelcard or, if you're using n Oyster Card, place it on the yellow-and-black Oyster reader in front of the river's compartment. This will beep and display a green light to show your card as been accepted. A couple of routes still use the classic Routemaster buses and ave old-fashioned uniformed conductors on board. Simply show your card when they ome round to check fares.

or the best view of London from the bus, head straight to the top deck. The front eats are the ones to try and grab but, if these are occupied, look for a window seat at doesn't have a support strut running down its centre. You don't want to have your ew obstructed. A few routes use single-decker buses. To maximise your view on ese, either stand up in the wide area on the left-hand side or go for the lower-level eats towards the front of the bus – you'll be able to see much more from these than om the raised ones at the back.

No 42
15
TOWER HILL

OFFICES
TO LET
PEARL & COUTTS
020 7843 3788
FOOD
& WINE
OPEN 24 HRS
EAT

Noose behind the Prospect of Whitby pub, Wapping, close to the site of Execution Dock

1. crime & punishment

Lawlessness has always been a characteristic of London life. And, in the days before the establishment of an effective police force, casual criminality was rife. For those scraping a living in the city's filthy slums, the money and status afforded by a life of crime was more than worth the threat of a spell in prison or even – in a world where few lived past 30 – dangling from the gallows. London's magnet-like status for itinerant provincial workers also guaranteed a regular supply of vulnerable souls to be preyed on by unscrupulous villains. And it's telling how many of the crimes highlighted in this journey were at the expense of those attempting to come to terms with the bewildering metropolis. London's landscape may have changed, but the grisly spectres of the past still stalk the city streets. You just need to know where to look.

Start point: Wapping overground
End point: Whitechapel tube
Duration: 4 hours

● Come out of **Wapping overground** and turn left down Wapping High Street. This docklands district still maintains the seafaring spirit of its 18th-century heyday and its association with pirates goes back to the 1500s. Turn left down King Henry's Stairs and walk along the bridge. The Captain Kidd pub, just downstream, is situated above the site of **Execution Dock**, which is where all pirates, smugglers and mutineers sentenced to death in London – including Kidd himself in 1701 – were hanged. Those who sailed under a skull and crossbones were reviled by Londoners, who relied on sea trade for much of their livelihood, so the punishment for piracy was particularly grim. A short rope meant victims suffered from slow strangulation rather than a broken neck and, as they were left hanging while three tides washed over their heads, most died from drowning.

● Walk back to **Wapping overground** and catch the westbound **100** bus from the stop right outside the exit. The bus turns left at **The Highway** – scene of the infamous Ratcliff Highway Murders in 1811, in which two families were slain in their own homes 12 days apart. The supposed murderer, a sailor lodging at a nearby pub, committed suicide before providing any kind of testimony, and his body was buried at the junction of Commercial Road and Cannon Street Road – just a few blocks northeast of here – with a stake driven through his heart.

● The bus continues past the **Tower of London**. The use of torture and axe-wielding executioners here has been much exaggerated, but both were certainly employed – most notably on 17th-century gunpowder plotter Guy Fawkes, who was subjected to the rack in order to gain a confession. King Henry VIII's wives Anne Boleyn and Catherine Howard, as well as 'nine days queen' Lady Jane Grey, were all beheaded within its walls. **Tower Hill**, just visible from the bus behind the tube station, was where the public executions of more than 100 prisoners were carried out.

● Get off the bus at the **St Paul's Station** stop, walk back up the street and turn left into Little Britain. Bear right when it meets King Edward Street and carry on along Little Britain as it passes through St Bartholomew's Hospital. You will emerge into **Smithfield**, where the open-air executions of heretics took place in medieval and Tudor times. Hundreds of religious dissenters were burnt at the stake

here, many of them during the reign of the zealous Mary I. Convicted 16th-century forgers suffered an equally gruesome fate – they were boiled alive in oil.

● Turn left across the front of the hospital and stop at the **memorial to Sir William Wallace**. This Scottish patriot – portrayed by Mel Gibson in *Braveheart* – met his end at Smithfield, too. As punishment for leading a rebellion against the English, he was dragged here through the streets by horses, then hung, drawn and quartered. His head was placed on London Bridge as a warning to other would-be traitors.

● Continue across the front of St Bartholomew's Hospital and walk down Giltspur Street. On the right, on the corner of Cock Lane, you will see the Golden Boy of Pye Corner. The statue was originally built into the wall of **The Fortune of War** pub, which was infamous for its connections with London's bodysnatchers. Surgeons at London's hospitals had always relied on the corpses of executed criminals for anatomical research, but as the numbers of those sentenced to death dwindled in the 18th and 19th centuries, there was a shortage of bodies to dissect. Into the breach stepped the resurrection men, who stole bodies from graves to sell on to doctors. At The Fortune of War, which stood here till 1910, corpses were laid out in the upstairs rooms for surgeons from nearby St Bartholomew's to purchase.

● Directly opposite the bottom of Giltspur Street is the **Old Bailey** central criminal court, which is built on the site of Newgate Prison. This notorious jail was the starting point for many a journey to the scaffold, and the route that condemned prisoners took can be followed by crossing the road at the bottom of Giltspur Street, turning right onto Holborn Viaduct and catching the westbound **8** from the **City Thameslink Station** stop. Carts transported those destined for the gallows to Tyburn – now Marble Arch – and the three-mile route would have been lined with onlookers, as well as food-sellers, ballad-hawkers and other tradesmen capitalising on the carnival-like atmosphere of a hanging day.

● Just after the bus passes Holborn tube station, look out for **The Princess Louise** pub on the left. This Victorian bar is one of the places in which serial killer **Dennis Nilsen** used to pick up his victims in the late 1970s and early 1980s. Nilsen targeted homeless men, students or itinerant workers, and took them back to his homes in Cricklewood and Muswell Hill, where he murdered them, cut them up and kept them beneath the floorboards.

● Get off the bus at the **Great Titchfield Street** stop and catch the westbound **7**. Just after it turns off Oxford Street, get off at the **Marble Arch/Edgware Road** stop and cross the road at the lights in front of the Odeon cinema. The island in the middle of the road is situated on the site of the **Tyburn Tree** gallows – a huge scaffold that allowed for mass executions. More than 40,000 people lost their lives on this spot between 1571 and 1783. A simple plaque set into the pavement is all that remains.

● Cross the road, turn left and catch the **23** bus from the identically named stop on the other side. Just before it turns off the Strand into Aldwych, look along the road for the purple flags that hang from **King's College**. It was to here in 1831 that bodysnatching gang the London Burkers brought the corpse of a 14-year-old boy to sell for dissection. When surgeons at the college realised it showed no signs of burial, they called in the police – who went on to uncover a grim tale of opportunism that saw the Burkers targeting lone provincial farmworkers on their way to Smithfield Market and drowning them in a well in order to sell the bodies.

● When the bus enters Fleet Street, look out for the Dundee Courier building at number 186. This is supposedly the site

yburn Tree plaque, Marble Arch

of 'the demon barber of Fleet Street' **Sweeney Todd's shop**. Whether or not Todd existed is uncertain – but the story of the hairdresser slitting his victims' throats with a razor and using their corpses to provide pie fillings for the next-door bakery has endured more than 200 years.

● Get off the bus at the **Fetter Lane** stop, walk back and turn right up Chancery Lane. Turn left into Carey Street then right up Serle Street, and you will find yourself in **Lincoln's Inn Fields**. This large green space was the site of several executions in the Renaissance period, most notably of the Babington plotters, who planned to assassinate Queen Elizabeth I. They were hung, drawn and quartered here in 1586.

● From Lincoln's Inn Fields, walk up Newman's Row on the far right of the square and through Great Turnstile onto High Holborn. Cross the road and catch the eastbound **25** from the **Brownlow Street** stop. As this heads out of the City and into Whitechapel, look out for Mitre Street on the left as the bus leaves Leadenhall Street and moves onto Aldgate. It was in **Mitre Square** – the entrance to which can be seen about halfway up here – that the mutilated body of Catherine Eddowes, the penultimate victim of serial killer Jack the Ripper, was found in November 1888.

● His first victim, Mary Ann Nichols, was found in Whitechapel, in August of that year. And you can visit the scene of the crime by getting off the bus at the **East London Mosque** stop. Continue on foot along Whitechapel Road, turn left into Vallance Road then right into **Durward Street.** It was on this road that the body of Nichols was discovered on the far side of the railway bridge, on the left-hand side. Despite a huge manhunt, four other women – possibly more – were slain in the area over the next few months. As the killer was never caught, the lurid speculation about the culprit's identity shows no sign of abating in the 21st century.

● At the end of Durward Street, turn right down Brady Street and left back onto Whitechapel Road. The first pub you come to, **The Blind Beggar**, was a haunt of gangsters in the 1950s and 1960s; and it was where Ronnie Kray, one half of the infamous Kray twins, sho dead rival George Cornell 1966 – a crime for which he was convicted and sentenced, along with his brother, to life imprisonment. Don't let this put you off marking the end of your journey with a pint in this atmospheric Victorian booze

To download this journey to your Smartphone, scan the QR code (right)

Marble Arch/
Edgware Road
Tyburn Tree
Great Titchfield Street
The Princess Louise
Sweeney Todd's shop
King's College
Lincoln's
Inn Fields
Fetter Lane
The Fortune of War
Smithfield
St Paul's Station
Newgate Prison
Mitre Square
Tower Hill
Tower of London
Buck's Row
The Blind Beggar
The East London Mosque
Commercial Road/
Cannon Street junction
Ratcliff Highway
Wapping overground
Execution Dock

2. ancient london

Hard though it is to imagine, London didn't really exist before the Romans arrived in 43AD. There is some evidence of Iron and Bronze Age villages in the area north of the River Thames and many historians think that Celtic druids would have performed ceremonies and rites on sacred mounds around the modern-day city centre. But it was only once the invading army under Emperor Claudius establishe the settlement of Londinium that the city as we know it began to take shape. The extensive wall the Romans built around this important strategic and trading post still exists in places and the gates they established live on in the names of streets and tube stations familiar to all Londoners. Glimpses of their civilisation – and those of the Saxons and Vikings who came afterwards – can still be seen in the modern city, as this journey shows you.

Start point: Angel tube
End point: Vauxhall tube
Duration: 4.5 hours

● Come out of **Angel tube** and turn left. Cross City Road and continue down St John Street, then turn right into Rosebery Avenue. The former headquarters of the London Water Board – on the right immediately after Sadler's Wells Theatre – sits on the site of **Penton Hill**, which is one of the three sacred mounds of Ancient London. This is where it is believed Celtic druids conducted rites in the centuries before the Romans arrived in 43AD.

● Either retrace your steps to Angel tube or catch the northbound **19, 38** or **341** from the **Sadler's Wells Theatre** stop back up to the **Angel Station** stop. When you recross City Road, you are passing over the intersection of two Bronze and Iron Age roads that were used to drive horses and cattle between modern-day Highgate and Covent Garden in one direction, and from here to what is now Highbury in the other. Though records of settlement in London only go back as far as the Roman era, these tracks suggest there were Celtic villages dotted around the area.

● Once you've got off the bus, cross the road and catch the southbound **30, 73** or **476** from the identically named stop on the other side. All these buses head down Pentonville Road to the **King's Cross Station** stop. It is thought that Boudicca, Queen of the Iceni, who led her tribe in a rebellion against the Roman occupiers in 60AD, was defeated close to modern-day King's Cross. Some historians have suggested that her body lies somewhere between platforms 9 and 10.

● Get off the bus at the King's Cross Station stop, walk back down Grays Inn Road and turn left up Caledonian Road. Cross Pentonville Road, continue up Caledonian Road, then catch the southbound **17** from the **King's Cross Station/Pentonville Road** stop. When the bus turns off Farringdon Street onto Ludgate Hill, look out for the plaque on the left that marks the location of the **Ludgate** – the westernmost gate in the Roman wall that was built around the settlement of Londinium in 200AD. The bus then continues past **St Paul's Cathedral**, first established in Saxon times by Mellitus, the first Christian bishop of London, in 604AD. According to contemporary reports, he built it on the site of a Roman temple to the Goddess Diana.

● When the bus heads along Cannon Street, look to the left as you pass number 111. Set into an alcove in the wall is the

London Stone – which, according to legend, is part of the original altar of the temple of Diana established by Brutus of Troy, who supposedly became the first King of England after he and his brother defeated the giant Gogmagog in a wrestling match. Legend has it that he established the city – which he called Troia Nova – around 1000BC. The stone is actually thought to be a Roman milestone or part of a druidic altar.

● **London Bridge**, which the bus crosses next, has existed in various forms since the Romans forded the river around 30 metres east of the current structure in the first century AD. It is believed to have been the location of a fierce battle between Anglo-Saxon settlers and Viking invaders led by Olaf II in the early 11th century. Though the Saxons occupied the bridge and rained spears down on those beneath, Viking longboats were tied to the bridge's supports and pulled the whole thing down. The discovery of iron axes and swords beneath this section of the Thames add weight to the theory that a mass slaughter did indeed take place here.

● Get off the bus at **London Bridge Station** and walk through the tube station to Duke Street Hill. Catch the eastbound **RV1** from the identically named stop and take the bus along Tooley Street and over Tower Bridge. Get off at **Tower Gateway**, walk back down Minories and turn right onto **Tower Hill**. This elevated spot – which roughly equates to the modern-day Trinity Square Gardens – is another of London's three sacred mounds. Referred to by early historians as the **White Mound**, it is a supposed druidic site. Remnants of a Bronze Age village have been found here, too. Tower Hill is also home to one of the best-preserved sections of the Roman wall that once completely encircled Ancient London and remained largely intact until as late as the 18th century.

● Walk through Trinity Square Gardens and bear right onto Cooper's Row. You can see another particularly well-preserved section of the Roman wall by entering **Trinity Court**, on the right. Continue up Cooper's Row and, at the top, turn right onto Crosswall. Cross Minories, walk along Portsoken Street and turn left up Mansell Street. Catch the westbound **100** from the **Mansell Street** stop. The bus takes you past the site of the **Aldgate** – the easternmost gate in the Roman wall – which stood at the corner of what's now Minories and Duke's Place, just after Aldgate tube.

● The 100 continues past Sir Norman Foster's iconic **30 St Mary Axe** building

ection of Roman wall, Trinity Court

(better-known as the Gherkin). During construction on the tower in 2003, builders came across human remains, which turned out to be the body of a teenage girl who had died in the Roman city some time between 350 and 400AD. Once the skyscraper was completed, her body was reburied according to Roman traditions and a headstone – incorporating both English and Latin inscriptions – was placed on the Bury Street side of the building.

● The bus continues along the road now called London Wall (which loosely follows the line of the original wall's northern section). Further sections of the Roman wall can be seen on the right, where Wood Street meets St Alphage Garden (which was also the site of **Cripplegate** – one of the original gates in the Roman wall); and on the left, where part of the fort that guarded the city defences is visible on Noble Street. **Aldersgate** – a gate added around 350AD – was situated where Aldersgate Street meets St Martin Le Grand, just after the bus turns left after passing the Museum of London.

● Get off the bus at the **City Thameslink Station/Ludgate Circus** stop, walk back along Ludgate Hill and turn left up Old Bailey. The junction with Newgate Street and Holborn Viaduct was the site of the **Newgate** – another of the wall's original gates – which was demolished in 1767.

● Turn right down Newgate Street, cross the road and catch the eastbound **8** from the **King Edward Street** stop. Get off at the **Wormwood Street** stop and continue up Bishopsgate until you arrive at the junction with Wormwood Street. This was the site of the **Bishopsgate** – another of the original gates – which marked the beginning of Ermine Street, the Roman Road that ran from here all the way to York. The gate's location is marked by a stone bishop's mitre, which is positioned high on the building that stands at the junction.

● Turn left down Wormwood Street and right up Old Broad Street, then take the westbound **11** from the **Liverpool Street Station** bus stop. Just after you pass the **Bank Station/Queen Victoria Street** stop, look left for a sight of the third-century **Roman Temple of Mithras**, which was relocated to Temple Court in the 1950s after being unearthed during building work. The temple contained several marble effigies of Roman gods and clay figurines of the goddess Venus, and nearb was found a small lead tablet on which someone had inscribed the name Martia

Detail from the Temple of Mithras, now held in the Museum of London

Martina backwards and thrown it into the River Walbrook as a way of summoning the gods to punish her. All these discoveries can be seen in the Museum of London.

● As the bus goes along Fleet Street, look left to see **St Bride's Church**. Though the current building is a 17th-century creation, there has been a Christian church here since the sixth century. This was built on top of a second-century structure that historians think was a temple associated with a sacred well – once dedicated to the Celtic fertility goddess Brigid – which still bubbles beneath the ground to the southeast of the church wall. The St Bride's crypt houses remains from this temple as well as a section of Roman pavement from a century or so earlier.

● When the bus moves onto the **Strand**, it is passing through the location of the Saxon settlement of **Lundenwic** – around a mile west of the original Roman city. This Thameside trading port stretched as far west as present-day Trafalgar Square and as far north as Oxford Street. Recent archaeological excavation around the church of St Martin-in-the-Fields – on the right-hand side just before the bus reaches Trafalgar Square – has unearthed Saxon graves dating from 500–650AD in which jewellery, as well as ceramic, glass and metal vessels were buried along with the deceased.

● Just before the bus reaches Victoria Station, look left to see the Catholic Westminster Cathedral. This has long been a spot associated with religion. It was a Benedictine priory until the time of the Reformation and, before that, it was the site of **Tothill** – the third of London's prehistoric sacred mounds.

● Get off the bus at the **Vauxhall Bridge Road/Victoria Station** stop, continue walking down the road and turn left down Vauxhall Bridge Road. Catch the southbound 2 from the Neathouse Place stop, which takes you over **Vauxhall Bridge**. If you are crossing the River Thames at low tide, look out for a huddle of poles and stumps sticking out of the mud in front of the MI6 Building (to the left of the bridge). A recent *Time Team* investigation revealed these are more than 6,000 years old, and were either supports for a walkway out to an island in the river or of ceremonial significance – a kind of small-scale, wooden stonehenge. They may not be the most impressive sight in the city, but they are by far the oldest.

To download this journey to your Smartphone, scan the QR code (right).

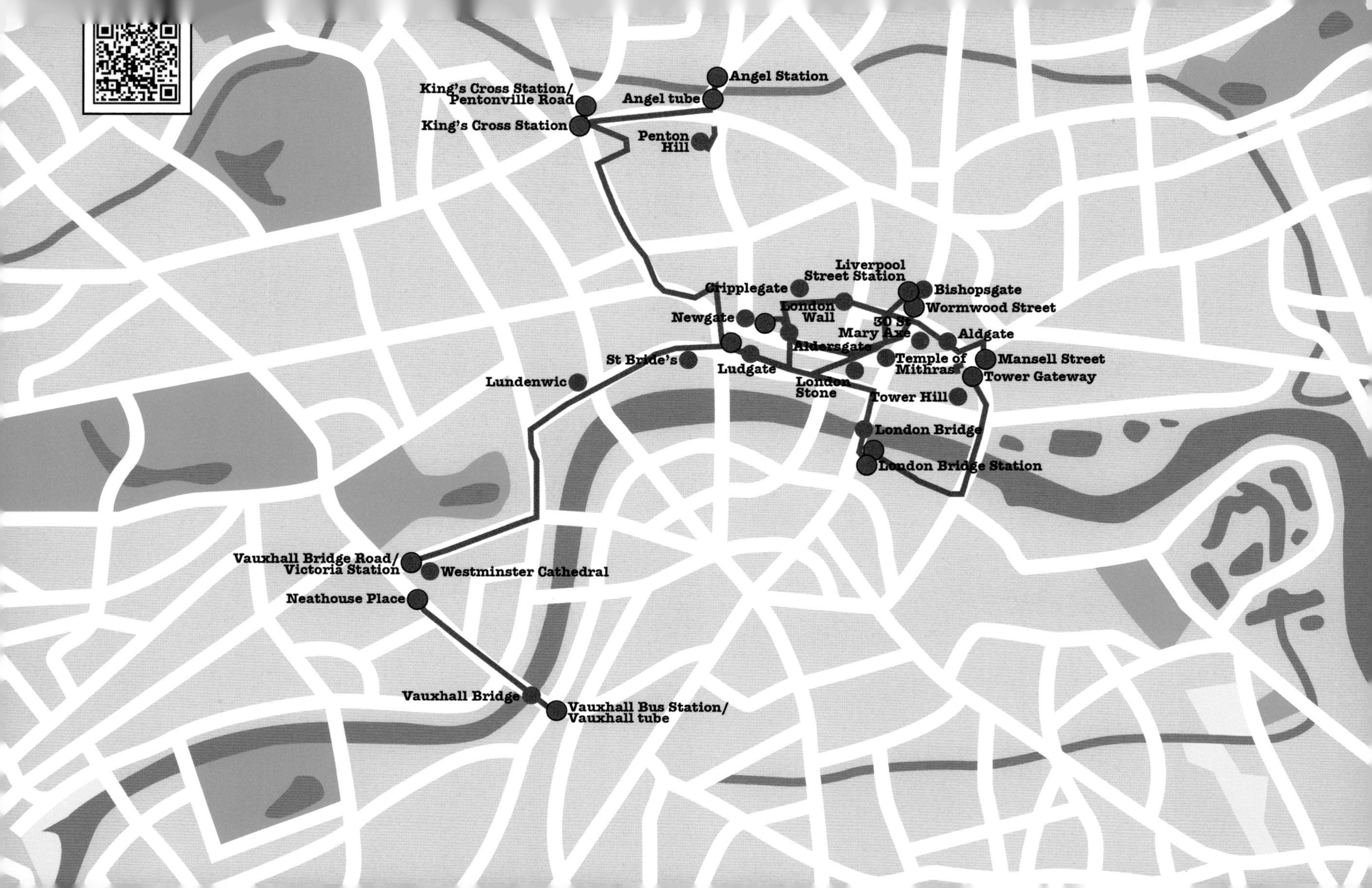
Angel Station
King's Cross Station/
Pentonville Road
Angel tube
King's Cross Station
Penton
Hill
Liverpool
Street Station
Cripplegate
Bishopsgate
London
Wall
Wormwood Street
Newgate
30 St
Mary Axe
Aldgate
Aldersgate
St Bride's
Temple of
Mithras
Mansell Street
Ludgate
Lundenwic
London
Stone
Tower Gateway
Tower Hill
London Bridge
London Bridge Station
Vauxhall Bridge Road/
Victoria Station
Westminster Cathedral
Neathouse Place
Vauxhall Bridge
Vauxhall Bus Station/
Vauxhall tube

3. babylon by bus

The arrival of the ship *MV Empire Windrush* at Essex's Tilbury Docks in 1948 is generally considered to be the start of modern multicultural London. On board were 492 Caribbean immigrants, who had responded to adverts in Jamaica that offered cheap transport to the UK for anyone wanting work. Once in London, many of these passengers stayed and settled with their families. And, over the following decades, these pioneers were joined by thousands of othe black immigrants from all over the Commonwealth, lured by the promise of better-paid jobs. It wasn't easy for these newcomers. The had to confront racism and prejudice – an issue that still regularly rears its head today – but, despite these problems, they adopted London as their home and gradually made certain districts their own Thanks to them, the capital is a far more vibrant and exciting place.

Electric Avenue, Brixton

Start point: Clapham South tube
End point: Ladbroke Grove tube
Duration: 4.5 hours

● **Clapham South tube** is home to one of London's eight deep-level air-raid shelters, which were built to protect locals from bombs during World War II. And, once the war ended, one more use was found for it. It was here that passengers from the *MV Empire Windrush* were housed by the Colonial Office when they first arrived in London from Jamaica. The first significant wave of Caribbean immigrants to arrive in the capital, they used the shelter as a base while they found jobs at the nearest labour exchange – situated on Coldharbour Lane in Brixton. This quirk of geography is the sole reason why Brixton became London's most recognisable West Indian district. Come out of the tube, cross the road and catch the eastbound **355** from the **Clapham South Station** stop.

● Get off the bus at the **Brixton Station** stop. For a taste of the area's unique Caribbean flavour, walk back on yourself and turn left into **Electric Avenue** to wander through the market, passing vegetable stalls, piles of household goods and the whole carcasses of dead chickens dangling at the front of butchers. It was outside the Iceland supermarket here that neo-Nazi David Copeland, who terrorised the capital in April 1999, left one of his three nailbombs – hoping the explosion would stimulate a race war.

● Turn right onto **Atlantic Road** from Electric Avenue. On the left-hand side is an entrance to the new **Brixton Market,** which is full of restaurants, coffee joints and quirky shops. At the end of Atlantic Road, turn right down **Coldharbour Lane**. You will emerge alongside the **Tate Library** (ironically bequeathed to a pre-West Indian Brixton by Caribbean sugar magnate and slave owner Henry Tate in 1892).

● This area has a history of rioting in modern times – behind you lies **Railton Road**, which was the frontline in the 198 Brixton race riots, while the Dogstar pub on Coldharbour Lane was burnt out and looted as part of the 1995 riots (locals resented the fact it had been changed from a traditional, black-owned pub into a trendy hangout for the white middle classes who were starting to move to the area). Turn right up Brixton Road from Coldharbour Lane and in five minutes you will pass **Brixton Police Station** on the right – this was the focus of the

community's anger in 1995 after a 26-year-old black man died in police custody there.

● Walk back down Brixton Road and take the left-hand fork into Effra Road. Catch the eastbound **37** from the **St Matthew's Church** bus stop – which is situated in front of **Windrush Square**, renamed in 1998 in tribute to the original 492 Caribbean immigrants who arrived in London 50 years before. The bus passes by Brockwell Park, one of London's hidden gems, and then through the well-to-do tree-lined suburbs of Herne Hill and East Dulwich before reaching the bustle of Peckham's Rye Lane, lined with hairdressers and stores selling cassava and yam.

● Get off the bus at the **Peckham Rye Station** stop and continue along Rye Lane. **Rye Lane Market**, a little bit further up on the left, is an indoor market that serves the West African community in this part of southeast London. Look out for the booths selling racily titled Nigerian DVDs, such as *Clash of the Lesbians 2*.

● Return to the **Peckham Rye Station** stop and catch the northbound **63** through Peckham's estates, the jaded flats of Elephant & Castle, over the River Thames (with views of St Paul's to your right) and into the business district of Farringdon. Get off the bus at the **Calthorpe Street** stop by a huge Royal Mail depot, carry on for a few metres up Farringdon Road, then turn left into Calthorpe Street. Continue straight ahead at all junctions and in around 15 minutes, after passing Goodenough College and along the back of Great Ormond Street Hospital, you will reach Russell Square. Turn left, walk around the bottom end of the square and across on to Montagu Place. Turn right up **Malet Street** and you will see a plaque dedicated to Mary Prince, the Bermudian abolitionist, whose unflinching autobiography *The History of Mary Prince* (published in 1831) did muc to change 19th-century attitudes toward slavery in the West Indies. She lived in the vicinity of this street after running away from her master while in London.

● At the end of Malet Street, turn left on to Torrington Place and then right up Gower Street. At the end, cross over Euston Road and catch the northbound **30** from the **Euston Square Station** bus stop, directly opposite the entrance to University College Hospital. The bus passes the red-brick slabs of the British Library and glorious facade of St Pancr Station, then goes through Angel and

frican shops at Ridley
oad Market, Dalston

along stylish Upper Street, before reaching Dalston. Get off the bus at the **Dalston Junction Station** stop. Carry on along the road for a few metres, then turn left. After 100 metres or so, you will see **Ridley Road Market** on your right, opposite Dalston Kingsland Station. The market is well-known in north London for its impressive selection of Caribbean and African goods. Expect to see barracuda, outlandish duvet sets and extravagantly named hairdressing salons.

● Return to Dalston Junction crossroads and continue walking down Kingsland Road. Catch the southbound **242** from the **Kingsland Road/Forest Road** stop. This takes you through trendy Shoreditch and back into London's financial district, where City workers scuttle into glass skyscrapers, clutching takeaway coffees.

● After turning right along Threadneedle Street and Cheapside, the bus passes St Paul's Cathedral and eventually reaches the West End and Oxford Street. Get off at the **Tottenham Court Road Station** stop and continue along St Giles High Street until it meets New Oxford Street. Turn left here and continue along Oxford Street, then turn left into Soho Street just after Tottenham Court Road tube. This leads into **Soho Square**, where Mary Seacole – recently voted the greatest-ever black Briton – lived at number 14. She was a Jamaican nurse who, in her lifetime, was as equally feted as Florence Nightingale for her medical achievements in the Crimean War. A blue plaque commemorates her on the front of the house.

● Return to Oxford Street, turn right and catch the westbound **7** from the **Oxford Street/Soho Street** bus stop. This takes you all the way to **Ladbroke Grove Station**, centre of the Notting Hill district that was London's other major centre of Caribbean immigration in the post-Windrush era. It was in this area that white landlord Peter Rachman became notorious for exploiting his new black tenants, charging them extortionate rates for tiny, squalid properties they had to accept, as racism prevented them from finding anything else locally. Like Brixton, Notting Hill has been the backdrop to major race riots – in 1958, when racist teddy boys attacked the homes and businesses of the fledgling community; and in 1976 following a skirmish at the Notting Hill Carnival. The world-famous carnival began as an attempt to improve race relations following the 1958 riots.

To download this journey to your Smartphone, scan the QR code (right)

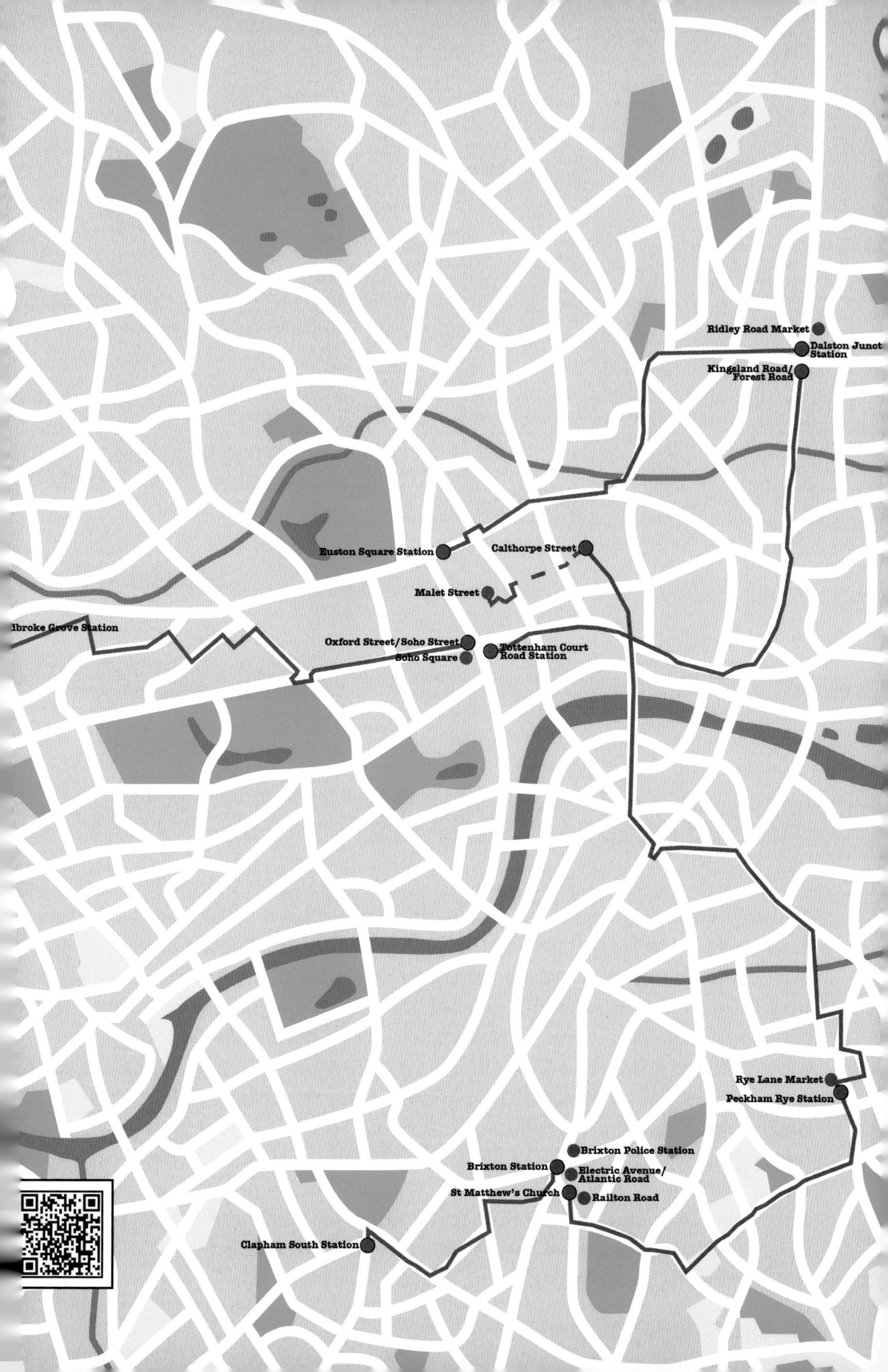

Ridley Road Market
Dalston Junct
Station
Kingsland Road/
Forest Road
Euston Square Station
Calthorpe Street
Malet Street
ibroke Grove Station
Oxford Street/Soho Street
Soho Square
Tottenham Court
Road Station
Rye Lane Market
Peckham Rye Station
Brixton Police Station
Brixton Station
Electric Avenue/
Atlantic Road
St Matthew's Church
Railton Road
Clapham South Station

4. the beatles' london

Though The Beatles were unquestionably a Liverpool band, London was their base from 1963 to 1970 – a period that coincided with them becoming the most famous group on the planet. John, Paul, George and Ringo relocated to the capital following the success of their first album *Please Please Me*, and became every bit as Metropolitan as they were Scouse. The band lived, worked and played in the districts around the Abbey Road studio where they recorded virtually all of their output. And, until their split, they were an integral part of London' legendary Swinging Sixties scene. This trip around The Beatles' capit haunts involves a couple of short walks in between bus journeys – th Soho and Mayfair streets that form much of their story are too narro for double-deckers, and the Midas-like wealth the band accumulated meant they tended to reside in exclusive areas, well away from traffi

Start point: St John's Wood tube
End point: Victoria tube
Duration: 3.5 hours

● Come out of **St John's Wood tube,** cross over the road, then turn left and walk down Wellington Road. At the hospital, turn right onto Circus Road then take the first left into **Cavendish Avenue.** Number seven, on the right, was Paul McCartney's home from 1966 onwards, and it was here that he wrote the songs *Yellow Submarine*, *Penny Lane* and *Hello Goodbye*, among others. He chose to live in this quiet road because of its proximity to The Beatles' recording studio, and you can recreate his walk to work by returning to Circus Road, turning left and then right up Grove End Road. After a few metres, this becomes **Abbey Road** – instantly recognisable from the zebra crossing over which the band strode on the cover of their penultimate album. EMI's **Abbey Road Studios,** in which The Beatles first auditioned for producer George Martin in 1962 and used to record almost all of their songs, is on the left.

● Walk up the opposite side of the road from the recording studio and catch the southbound **139** or **189** bus from the **Marlborough Place** stop. As the bus heads onto Baker Street, it passes the **former Apple Boutique** at number 94 on the left. A 'beautiful place for beautiful people to buy beautiful things' according to Paul McCartney, this ill-fated store – which is now a branch of Reed recruitment consultants, but was once covered in a lurid psychedelic mural – was opened by The Beatles in December 1967. It closed six months later after the band's laid-back approach to security led to widespread shoplifting and huge financial losses.

● Get off the bus at the **George Street** stop and catch the southbound **13**. As the bus leaves Baker Street and enters Portman Square, look left down Fitzhardinge Street, which has a branch of Barclays Bank on the corner. The modern, pale-brown building on the edge of Manchester Square is built on the spot of **EMI's former headquarters.** It was on the staircase here that The Beatles' famous 'red' and 'blue' covers (the ones in which the band looks down from a balcony) were taken in 1962 and 1969.

● As the 13 bus turns into Regent Street, you can see the Art Deco façade of **Broadcasting House** on the left. The Beatles recorded more than 50 radio programmes for the BBC in this iconic building as they cemented their reputation as the most exciting band of the early 1960s. The neoclassical building that now houses the Believe It Or Not Museum – directly in front of you as the bus nears the bottom of Regent Street – was once the **London Pavilion cinema**. It was here that the films *A Hard Day's Night*, *Help!* and *Yellow Submarine* all premiered, drawing huge, traffic-stopping crowds, which filled Piccadilly Circus. Look left to see **The Prince of Wales Theatre** as the bus turns down Haymarket. This was where John Lennon infamously entreated the royal family to 'rattle your jewellery' during the 1963 Royal Variety Performance.

● Get off the bus at the **Haymarket** stop, cross the road and walk along Charles II Street. Go through St James's Square, onto King Street and turn right up Duke Street St James's. **Mason's Yard** – the entrance to which is tucked away on the right just before The Chequers pub – was the home of the Scotch of St James club, in which The Beatles would drink and socialise with fellow musicians and other 1960s scenesters. Mason's Yard is most famous, though, as the place in which John Lennon first met Yoko Ono at an exhibition of her work in November 1966. **The Indica Gallery**, which hosted the show, was at number six.

● Continue on foot up Duke Street St James's. At the top, turn right onto Piccadilly, cross the road and head up Sackville Street. Bear left at the end of the road and turn right into **Savile Row**. This is where Apple – the record company set up by The Beatles – had its offices at number three. It was on the rooftop here that the band played live together for the last time in 1969 – blasting out *Get Back* to a bemused crowd on the street below.

● Carry on walking up Savile Row, turn right into New Burlington Street and cross busy Regent Street. Go down narrow Tenison Court directly opposite and you will emerge in front of number nine **Kingly Street**, once home to the Bag O'Nails club – a favourite drinking den of The Beatles. As the blue plaque inside the doorframe states, this is where Paul McCartney – who had his own VIP table at the venue – first met wife-to-be Linda Eastman at a gig.

● Turn right here, then left onto Beak Street. Walk right to the end and turn left onto Lexington Street. Go right at **Broadwick Street** and walk towards The

laque at 34 Montagu
quare, Marylebone

Blue Posts pub. The railings-surrounded public toilets on the left were used in a 1966 *Not Only... But Also* sketch in which John Lennon played a doorman guarding 'London's most fashionable lavatory' – and wore his trademark wire-framed glasses publicly for the first time.

● Continue along Broadwick Street, cross Wardour Street and bear left into needle-thin alleyway **St Anne's Court**. As well as being the scene of The Beatles' first London gig at the long-gone Blue Gardenia club – which may or may not have been at number 20 (no one seems to remember) – this tiny strip was also home to **Trident Studios**. Located at number 17, this then-state-of-the-art facility was where the band recorded the songs *Hey Jude*, *Martha My Dear* and *Dear Prudence*, among others, while they were waiting for EMI to upgrade the technology at Abbey Road.

● At the end of St Anne's Court, turn left and walk up Dean Street until you emerge on Oxford Street. Turn left, walk to the **Wardour Street** bus stop and catch the westbound **25**. Just before it reaches Oxford Circus tube, the bus passes across the top of Argyll Street. The entrance to **The London Palladium**, at which The Beatles performed for a live TV show in October 1963, can be seen on the left. The size of the crowd that filled Argyll Street that evening and the chaotic scenes that followed led to the first use of the term 'Beatlemania' in the morning newspapers.

● When the 25 bus terminates on **Holles Street**, walk onwards to Cavendish Square and bear left around it. Turn left at Wigmore Street and then right up **Wimpole Street**. Walk on for a few minutes and you will find yourself outside number 57, the house belonging to Paul McCartney's actress girlfriend Jane Asher that he moved into in 1964. *Yesterday* was written upstairs, while the basement is where McCartney and John Lennon worked on *I Want To Hold Your Hand*.

● Retrace your steps down Wimpole Street and turn right onto New Cavendish Street. Follow this to Marylebone High Street, then bear left across the road and continue along George Street for around 10 minutes before turning right into **Montagu Square**. Number 34, in the far corner, is where John Lennon lived with Yoko Ono after the collapse of his first marriage. It was at this property, owned by Ringo Starr, that the couple were arrested for marijuana possession in 1968.

● Walk straight up Upper Montagu Street from John and Yoko's flat and cro

Graffiti recreation of the Abbey oad album cover, on the wall of ne studio in which it was recorded

busy Marylebone Road. Bear left towards **Marylebone Station**, walk up Great Central Street and catch the southbound **2** bus from outside the railway terminus. This takes you past the pillared façade of **Marylebone Registry Office**, where Paul McCartney married Linda Eastman in 1969, on the right. Stay on the bus till the **Marble Arch Station** stop.

● Continue on foot down Park Lane for a few seconds and turn left into **Green Street**. At the far end, on the right, is number 57 in which all four Beatles lived together when they moved to London in 1963. Though they soon went their separate ways – Paul McCartney to Wimpole Street with Jane Asher, John Lennon and his wife Cynthia to a now-demolished building in West London, George Harrison and Ringo Starr to Knightsbridge – this was the band's base while they first got to know the capital. Less than two years later, only Paul remained in London; the other three preferring the relative anonymity of the Surrey countryside.

● Return to the **Marble Arch Station** bus stop and catch the southbound **73** to **Victoria Station**, which takes you along the eastern edge of **Hyde Park** – where the autumnal cover of the *Beatles For Sale* album was shot. As the bus continues down Park Lane, it passes **The London Hilton on Park Lane** on the left. This hotel is where transcendental meditation guru Maharishi Mahesh Yogi held a 1967 lecture that all four Beatles attended. Impressed by his vision, they later accompanied him to a meditation retreat in Rishikesh, India – an intensely creative period that saw the band write the majority of songs for *The Beatles*, the double LP more commonly known as the White Album.

● As the 73 rounds the arch at Duke of Wellington Place and heads along the edge of the gardens of **Buckingham Palace** – where The Beatles received their MBEs from the Queen in 1965 – look to the right for a glimpse of **Chapel Street**. This smart Belgravia enclave is where the band's manager Brian Epstein lived at number 24. Depressed and increasingly reliant on drugs (both prescription and recreational), he died here from an accidental overdose in August 1967, plunging The Beatles into an internal power struggle that led to their implosion a couple of years later.

To download this journey to your Smartphone, scan the QR code (right).

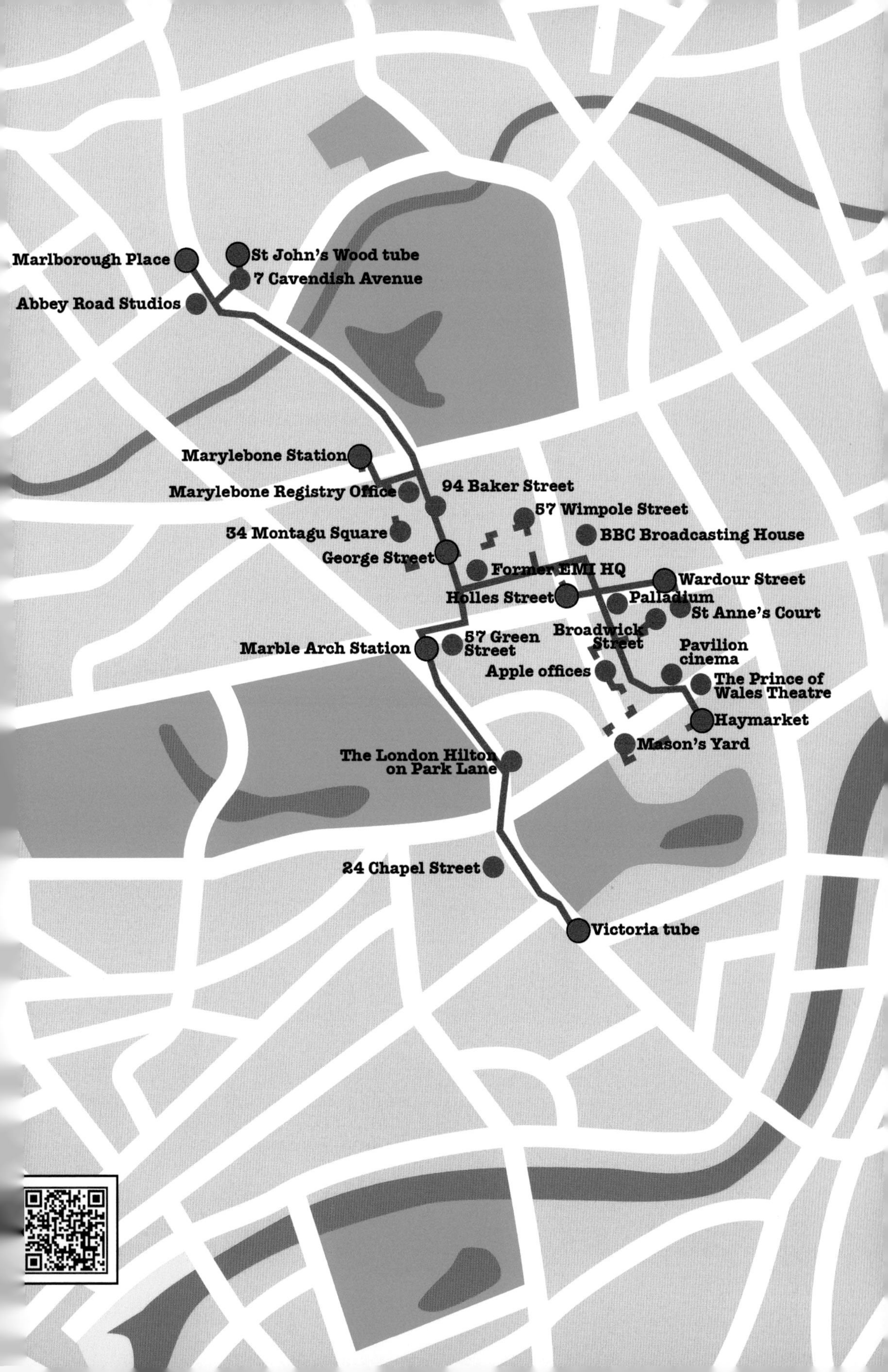
Marlborough Place
St John's Wood tube
7 Cavendish Avenue
Abbey Road Studios
Marylebone Station
Marylebone Registry Office
94 Baker Street
57 Wimpole Street
34 Montagu Square
BBC Broadcasting House
George Street
Former EMI HQ
Wardour Street
Holles Street
Palladium
St Anne's Court
Broadwick Street
Marble Arch Station
57 Green Street
Pavilion cinema
Apple offices
The Prince of Wales Theatre
Haymarket
Mason's Yard
The London Hilton on Park Lane
24 Chapel Street
Victoria tube

Hackney Marshes

5. this sporting life

A sporting city to rival anywhere in the world, London – home of the 2012 Olympics – takes the physical battle very seriously indeed. Its 32 boroughs are home to 14 professional football clubs, watched by hundreds of thousands of people each week, as well as two test cricketing counties and countless other teams across a variety of disciplines. Its stadiums and complexes, spread out over the city to serve its distinct communities, host everyone from world-famous brands – Arsenal, Chelsea, the Wimbledon Championships – to local athletics clubs and amateur teams. And wherever you go in the city (and on this marathon journey, you'll visit much of it), you will see goalposts, basketball nets or racing tracks set up for the next generation of sportsmen and women to hone their talent. The Olympic torch couldn't have come to a more appropriate place.

Start point: Southfields tube
End point: St John's Wood tube
Duration: 7.5 hours

● Come out of **Southfields tube,** cross the road and turn right down Wimbledon Park Road. Catch the southbound **493** and get off at the **Wimbledon Tennis Club & Museum** stop for **The All England Lawn Tennis & Croquet Club.** This club has hosted the Wimbledon Championships, the world's oldest and most prestigious tennis tournament, since 1877. Though it's now a mega complex comprising two stadium-like show courts, 17 tournament courts and hi-tech facilities, it is still a bastion of tradition. Sponsorship and advertising are conspicuous by their absence, players must wear white on court, and the occupants of Centre Court's Royal Box are always bowed or curtsied to. The club also hosted the tennis competition in the London 2012 Olympics.

● Walk back up Church Road and turn left into Victoria Drive. Catch the northbound **39** from the **Church Road** stop to **Putney/St Mary's Church,** which is situated on **Putney Bridge** – the starting point for the annual Oxford and Cambridge Boat Race. Continue walking over the bridge and take a short ride on the northbound **74, 220** or **430** from the **Putney Bridge/Gonville Road** stop on the other side of the river.

● Get off the bus at the **Bishops Park Road** stop and continue walking up Fulham Palace Road, then turn left into Finlay Street. **Fulham FC's Craven Cottage** stadium is situated at the other end. This charming, late 19th-century construction is the work of Scottish architect Archibald Leitch, who designed the cottage pavilion that gives the grounc its name, and has been designated a Grade II-listed building. One of London's six (at the time of writing) Premier League football clubs, Fulham FC may not be as illustrious as its near-neighbours Chelsea, or the North London giants Arsenal and Spurs, but it can boast perhaps the loveliest ground in the sport – plus one of the game's most eccentric owners in ex-Harrod's boss Mohammed Al Fayed.

● Turn right at the ground and walk along the back of the Johnny Haynes Stand – named after the ex-Fulham player and England captain – and catch the westbound **424** from the **Stevenage Road/Fulham Football Club** stop. This route is only operational from Monday t Saturday, so if you're doing this journey c a Sunday, retrace your steps down Fulha Palace Road and catch the westbound

Statue of Johnny Haynes outside Fulham FC's Craven Cottage stadium

414 from the **Fulham High Street** stop instead. Get off at **Fulham Broadway** and take the westbound **211** from the same stop. Almost immediately, the bus passes **Chelsea FC's Stamford Bridge** stadium on the left. This glitzy construction – which incorporates shops, restaurants, bars and a hotel – started life as another Archibald Leitch construction in 1877, but now reflects the club's Premier League and European success in recent years.

● Get off the bus at the **Victoria Station/ Grosvenor Gardens** stop and cross over to the other side of Buckingham Palace Road. Continue along the road and turn right into Victoria Street. After a few minutes, turn right down Vauxhall Bridge Road and catch the southbound **36, 185** or **436** from the **Neathouse Place** stop. All buses cross the River Thames and pass **The Oval** cricket ground on the left. Home of Surrey County Cricket Club, the stadium – which dates back to 1845 – hosts the final match of England's summer test series each year. It was also the venue for the world's first-ever international football match (a 1-1 draw between England and Scotland in 1870), as well as being the home of the FA Cup Final from 1872 to 1892.

● Get off the bus at the **Oval Station** stop, cross the road and catch the northbound **36** up to **Hyde Park Corner.** Continue on foot up Duke of Wellington Place and cross over Knightsbridge so that you're on the same side of the road as **Hyde Park** – venue for the triathlon and open-water swimming events at the London 2012 Olympics. Turn left and walk down the road for a minute or so, then catch the northbound **19** from the **Hyde Park Corner Station** stop up to **Museum Street.**

● Take the eastbound **25** from the same stop all the way to **Stratford Bus Station,** passing the **Olympic Stadium** – constructed for the 2012 games – and the **Olympic Park**, which houses many venues built especially for 2012, including the **Aquatics Centre** and **London Velopark.** The whole park is towered over by the 115-metre, helter skelter-like *Orbit*, which is the largest piece of public art in the UK.

● Take the northbound **308** from **Stratford Bus Station** to the **Homerton High Street/Hackney Hospital** stop facing Glyn Road. Though this journey is not a pretty one, it is a reminder why this area – one of the poorest districts in the country and in desperate need of investment – was chosen as the setting for the 2012 Olympics. En route, you will pass the northern part of the **Olympic**

Olympic Stadium, Stratford

Park and **Hackney Marshes** – home to more than 80 football pitches, and the heart of London's amateur football scene.

● Catch the northbound **236** from the same stop all the way to **Finsbury Park Station**. Just after the bus passes Highbury Fields, look to the left for a view of **Highbury stadium**, the former home of Arsenal FC. Now a complex of luxury flats, the Art Deco ground was originally designed by Archibald Leitch in 1913, but significantly developed during the 1930s. As well as being Arsenal's home until 2006, the stadium also played host to several other sports – including a 1966 World Heavyweight boxing title fight between Henry Cooper and Muhammad Ali.

● When the bus terminates at **Finsbury Park Station**, walk down the tunnel marked London Underground. At the other end, turn right and, once outside, catch the westbound **210**. As the bus heads towards Archway tube, you can catch glimpses of **Arsenal FC's Emirates Stadium** – the Premier League club's enormous, futuristic new home – on the left. But the best views are as the bus climbs Highgate Hill. After passing through Golders Green, the 210 turns left onto Highfield Avenue, which provides the first sight of **Wembley Stadium**. This 90,000-capacity arena – Europe's second-largest – is the home of the national football team, as well as the venue for all of the sport's major cup finals. It also hosts rugby, American football and other sporting events.

● When the bus route ends at **Brent Cross Shopping Centre**, continue around the bus station and catch the southbound **189** down to **St John's Wood Road/ Lord's Cricket Ground**. Once you get off, continue walking down Grove End Road and turn left into St John's Wood Road, passing **Lord's**, the famous cricket arena that has stood on this site since 1814. Home of the Marylebone Cricket Club – which established the rules of modern cricket in the 18th century – the stadium is also the base of Middlesex County Cricket Club, and is used by the English national side for the first match in its home test series every summer. A stunning combination of Victorian and cutting-edge modern architecture, it is undoubtedly the most famous cricket ground in the world and a fitting place to end your journey around London's sporting landmarks. **The Lord's Tavern** on St John's Wood Road is a good place to stop for a celebratory drink.

To download this journey to your Smartphone, scan the QR code (right)

Finsbury Park Station
Wembley Stadium
Highbury Stadium
Arsenal FC
Hackney Marshes
Homerton High Street/
Hackney Hospital
Stratford
Bus Station
Olympic Stadium
and Olympic Park
St John's Wood tube
Lord's
St John's Wood Road/
Lord's Cricket Ground
Museum Street
Hyde Park
Hyde Park
Corner Station
Hyde Park Corner
Victoria Station/
Grosvenor Gardens
Neathouse Place
The Oval
Oval tube
Chelsea FC
Fulham
Broadway
Stevenage Road/
Fulham Football Club
Fulham FC
Bishops Park Road
Putney/St
Mary's Church
Southfields tube
Wimbledon
Church Road

6. rhyme & reason

Look behind the inane, child-pleasing lyrics to nursery rhymes and you'll find something altogether darker. Developed in a time before mass communication, and before most people could read or write, these seemingly innocent ditties, invented and passed on by everyday people, are often a folk memory of important historical happenings; a carefully coded satire on the failings – both moral and political – of the ruling classes. London, the heartbeat of English life, reveals its face time and again in these songs, just as a journey around the older parts of the capital throws up glimpses of the centuries-old events that inspired them. With its oranges and lemons, and pudding pie and tuppenny rice, the city offers up more than enough fodder to feed the imagination of anyone who's ever found themselves humming these timeless tunes.

Start point: Westminster tube
End point: Old Street tube
Duration: 3.5 hours

● Exit **Westminster tube,** cross the river and catch the northbound **159** or **453** bus from the **Westminster Bridge/ County Hall** stop directly opposite the Marriott County Hall hotel. Almost immediately, you will pass the **Houses of Parliament** on the left. Though the current building is largely a 19th-century construction, the chambers within are the subject of the nursery rhyme *Remember, Remember, The Fifth of November*, which recalls the gunpowder plot of 1605. This attempt by Catholic terrorists to assassinate the Protestant King James I and his ministers by igniting gunpowder beneath the room in which they were meeting was foiled only at the last minute. The man caught trying to light the fuse – the now infamous Guy Fawkes – was hung, drawn and quartered, and had his body parts displayed throughout London to deter other would-be insurgents. His effigy continues to be burnt on pyres all over the UK on 5 November (Bonfire Night) each year.

● The bus turns right onto Whitehall, passing the Prime Minister's Downing Street home on the left on its way up to Trafalgar Square. The ghost of King Charles I hangs heavy over this area, and **Whitehall Palace,** outside which he was executed in 1645, can be seen on the right opposite the Horse Guards army headquarters. The statue of the King riding a horse at the top of Whitehall is on the spot of the original Charing Cross – one of 12 stone crosses erected by King Edward I between 1291 and 1294. It is a reminder of the nursery rhyme *As I Was Going By Charing Cross*, which recalls this act of Civil War regicide.

● When the bus turns left along Cockspur Street and Pall Mall, look out for **Carlton House Terrace** – two rows of white stucco-fronted houses on either side of the Duke of York column – on the left. These were built in the early 19th century on the site of Carlton House, which was the London residence of the Prince Regent, later King George IV. Known for his decadent lifestyle and numerous affairs, the famously fat monarch was the subject of the nursery rhyme *Georgie Porgie Pudding and Pie*. And it was here that 'he kissed the girls and made them cry'; misery-struck women in his life included disowned queen Caroline of Brunswick (who George didn't even allow to attend his coronation) and unacknowledged wife

Maria Anne Fitzherbert, not to mention the many unlucky ladies who were the subject of his sweaty advances.

● Get off at the **Regent Street/Charles II Street** stop, cross the road and walk for a couple of minutes up Charles II Street, emerging alongside Her Majesty's Theatre. Cross the road and catch the eastbound **15** bus from the **Haymarket** stop, which takes you past Charing Cross station on the right and a Victorian recreation of Edward I's original cross. The bus continues along the Strand and turns into Aldwych. Just after you pass the Waldorf Hotel, you'll get a glimpse of **Drury Lane** on your left. This is the home of The Muffin Man from the early 19th-century nursery rhyme. The Theatre Royal Drury Lane is also where, in 1779, King George 'Georgie Porgie' IV first set eyes on actress Mary Robinson, a woman whose reputation and career he destroyed with their very public affair. She no doubt had a good cry after that.

● After emerging from Aldwych, the bus heads along Fleet Street. As soon as you pass the griffin statue in the centre of the road (the boundary between the City of London and Westminster), look to the right to see **Ye Olde Cock Tavern**. In the mid-18th century, the original pub was located on the other side of the road and employed a barmaid called Lucy Locket. As recounted in the nursery rhyme, she lost her 'pocket' – 18th-century slang for a wealthy and generous lover – to notorious society beauty and courtesan Kitty Fisher. It gets worse for Lucy. The final lines, 'not a penny was there in it, but a ribbon round it' are incredibly loaded; prostitutes of the time would keep their ill-gotten gains tied in a ribbon around their thigh.

● As the 15 continues along Cannon Street, look out for the coffee house on the corner of Martin Lane to the right. The church of **St Martin Orgar** can be seen further down this street. This 15th-century chapel is the home of the 'bells of St Martin's' in the nursery rhyme *Oranges and Lemons*, which traces the journey of a condemned prisoner through London's streets to their execution at Tyburn. The first death knell to toll in the rhyme comes from 'the bells of St Clement's', which are in the church of **St Clement Eastcheap** on Clement's Lane. After passing Martin Lane, look to the left up King William Street for a glimpse of this medieval building.

● Look right just before you pass Monument tube station and you'll catch sight of **London Bridge** at the end of the street. Subject of one of the world's mos

St Clement Eastcheap,
Clement's Lane

famous nursery rhymes, London Bridge has fallen down and been rebuilt several times since the Romans first forded the River Thames in 60AD. While the verses of the rhyme – 'build it up with wood and clay', etc – refer to the building methods used by successive generations of Londoners, it is the repetition of 'my fair lady' that is most interesting. Could this be a reference to the young woman who was supposedly sacrificed and buried in the bridge's foundations back in the 12th century?

● The second road on the right after Monument tube provides the origins of another famous nursery rhyme. It was in a bakery on **Pudding Lane** that the Great Fire of London began in 1666 – the ensuing blaze, which razed the city to the ground, is remembered in *London's Burning* – sung by schoolchildren all over the English-speaking world.

● As the bus leaves Eastcheap and continues along Great Tower Street, the **Tower of London** can be seen directly ahead. After passing this ancient fortification – upon which the head of gunpowder plotter Guy Fawkes was displayed on a spike following his grisly execution – the bus loops around Aldgate and makes its way along Commercial Road into the East End district of Stepney. Get off the bus at the **Stepney Methodist Church** stop.

● Continue walking along Commercial Road for a minute or so, then turn left up Bromley Street. Head straight up the road and bear right at Stepney City Farm onto Stepney High Street. On the right you will see the 10th-century church of **St Dunstan & All Saints**, from which ring 'the bells of Stepney' in *Oranges and Lemons*. At the top of Stepney High Street, either bear left onto White Horse Lane and follow it for 10 minutes up to Mile End Road or take the northbound **309** from the **Stepney Green School** stop.

● Once on Mile End Road, catch the westbound **25** bus from opposite **Stepney Green tube**. On its way back into the City, the bus passes the **Whitechapel Bell Foundry**, which is on the left just after the enormous East London Mosque. Located here since 1570 the foundry cast the Liberty Bell and the bells of Big Ben, and replaced many of the medieval bells featured in *Oranges and Lemons* after the churches that held them were damaged in World War II.

● After passing the Royal Exchange on the corner of Cornhill and Threadneedle

itechapel Bell Foundry

Street, the bus heads up Cheapside and passes the church of **St Mary-le-Bow** ('the great bell of Bow') on the left. Another church to be featured in *Oranges and Lemons*, **St Sepulchre Without Newgate** ('the bells of Old Bailey'), can be seen on the right. This 12th-century church, which faces the former Newgate Prison (now The Old Bailey central criminal court) would toll its bells as condemned prisoners left the jail and headed to the gallows.

● Get off the bus at the **City Thameslink Station** stop and walk back over Holborn Viaduct before turning right down Old Bailey. Walk past the courthouse to the bottom of the road and turn left onto **Ludgate Hill**. Catch the eastbound **26** bus from the stop opposite Lloyds TSB bank, and head northeast through the City past St Paul's Cathedral and Liverpool Street Station. As the bus leaves the gleaming City behind and makes its way into scuffed and arty Shoreditch, it passes the final church to feature in *Oranges and Lemons* on the right. **St Leonard's** ('the bells of Shoreditch'), now something of an island in the midst of several busy roads, has stood on this site since the Dark Ages.

● Get off the bus at the **Hoxton Station** stop and carry on walking up the street. Following signs to Hoxton Station, turn left along Cremer Street and walk for a couple of minutes, passing the station on your right, before emerging on Kingsland Road. Turn right here and catch the westbound **394** from outside the **Geffrye Museum** – one of London's quirkier exhibition spaces, which is dedicated to the history of the English domestic interior.

● There's no pretending that the 394 bus route is a pretty one. The short journey takes you through some of North London's most depressing housing estates. However, it only takes 10 minutes for the bus to emerge on Shepherdess Walk, where you get off at the **Shoreditch Police Station** stop and walk down to **The Eagle** pub. Once a Victorian music hall, the pub – set back from City Road – is immortalised in the 'up and down the City Road, in and out The Eagle' lines of *Pop Goes the Weasel*. This 19th-century song, celebrating the legendary drunkenness of the area's silk weavers, is a fitting soundtrack to the end of the journey. Enjoy a pint in The Eagle (now an upmarket gastropub) before turning left along City Road and walking for a few minutes to Old Street tube.

To download this journey to your Smartphone, scan the QR code (right).

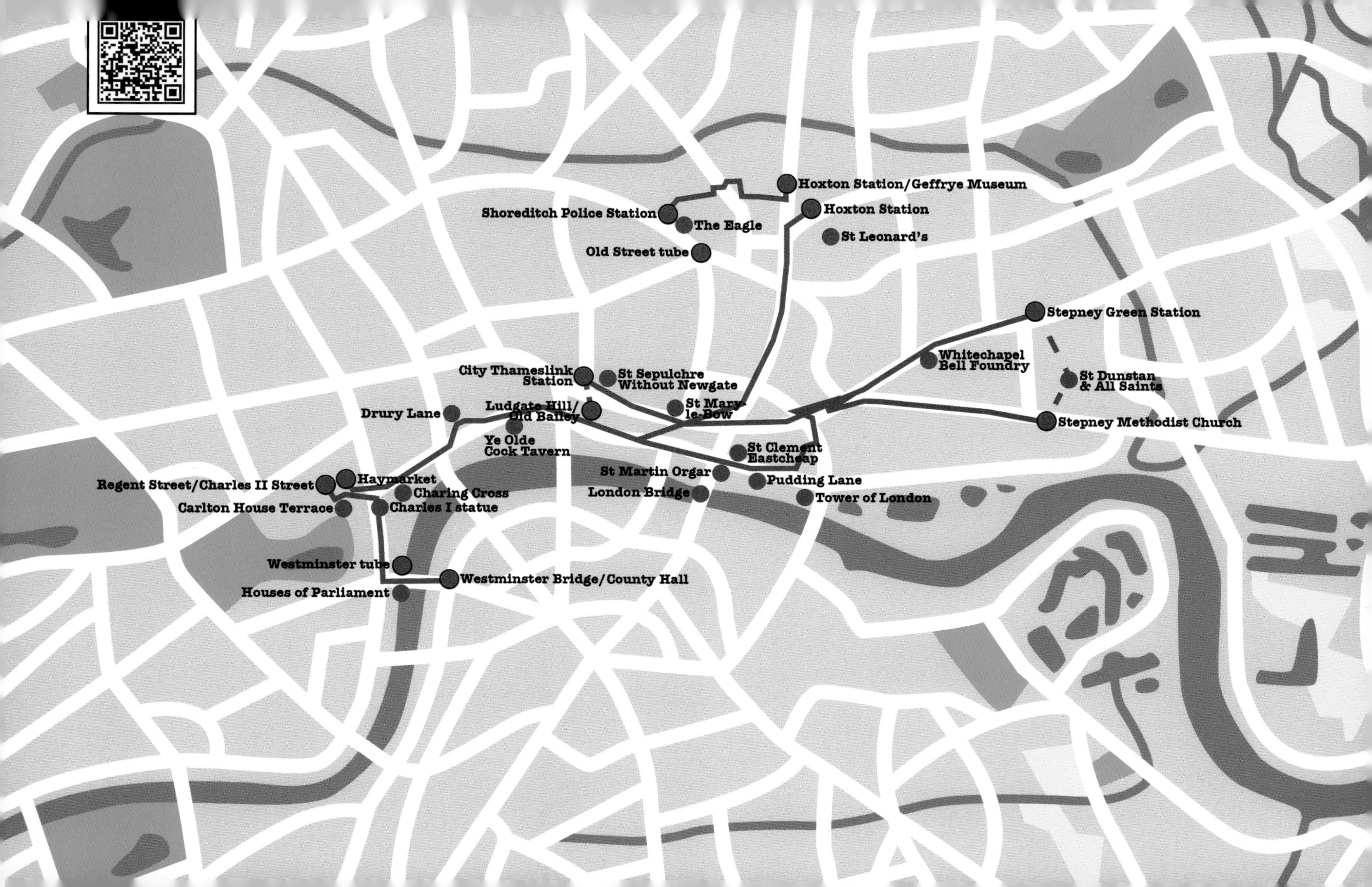
Hoxton Station/Geffrye Museum
Shoreditch Police Station
Hoxton Station
The Eagle
St Leonard's
Old Street tube
Stepney Green Station
Whitechapel Bell Foundry
City Thameslink Station
St Sepulchre Without Newgate
St Dunstan & All Saints
St Mary-le-Bow
Drury Lane
Ludgate Hill/Old Bailey
Stepney Methodist Church
Ye Olde Cock Tavern
St Clement Eastcheap
St Martin Orgar
Haymarket
Pudding Lane
Regent Street/Charles II Street
Charing Cross
London Bridge
Tower of London
Carlton House Terrace
Charles I statue
Westminster tube
Westminster Bridge/County Hall
Houses of Parliament

7. global london

London is a city of immigrants. While many of those – this writer included – came from Britain's provinces in search of work and greater opportunities, there are almost as many people living in the city who were born under a foreign flag, and raise families that strive to keep their community's identity alive. The most visible groups in London are the African, Caribbean, Asian and Jewish populations (all covered in more detail elsewhere in this book), but there are countless other smaller communities – from the Portuguese in Stockwell to the Greeks in Palmers Green – that make up the capital's vibrant cultural patchwork. Different countries and continents shape the unique atmosphere in every London postcode, so why not go around the world on your travelcard?

Start point: Stockwell tube
End point: Palmers Green overground
Duration: 4.5 hours

● Come out of **Stockwell tube**, cross the road and walk around the front of The Swan pub onto Stockwell Road. Catch the northbound **2** from the **Stockwell Gardens** stop, a few metres further down the road. The bus takes you along **South Lambeth Road** – known as Little Portugal. Portuguese immigrants first arrived here in the 1960s and 1970s to escape poverty and being conscripted to fight unpopular wars in their country's African colonies. The streets around South Lambeth Road are home to the largest Portuguese community outside Portugal, and the brightly decorated cafés, tapas bars and social clubs, many flying the national colours of red and green, reveal the strong Latin influence in this formerly run-down part of south London. To sample some of the best custard tarts in the area, stop off at Lisboa Patisserie at number 147; if you're passing through at lunchtime, check out Grelha d'Ouro, the locals' restaurant of choice, at number 151.

● Once the bus crosses Vauxhall Bridge and passes Hyde Park, get off at the **Marylebone Station** terminus. Continue along Melcombe Place and Harewood Row, then turn right up Lisson Grove. After a few metres, turn left into Bell Street and walk right to the end, passing the first few Middle Eastern businesses – cafés, grocers, travel agents that specialise in trips to the Hajj – which hint at this district's ethnic make-up. Arabs started settling around **Edgware Road** in the late 19th century as Britain strengthened its trade links with the Ottoman Empire; and further immigration followed in the 1950s – when many Egyptians arrived – and the 1970s and 1980s, after the outbreak of civil war in Lebanon and the overthrow of the Shah in Iran. Turn left onto Edgware Road and walk down the road to the **Sussex Gardens** bus stop. Catch the eastbound **7**, which takes you down Edgware Road, past the Lebanese restaurants, financial institutions and shisha cafes that make this section of old Roman road feel like a suburb of Beirut or Cairo. If you're hungry, pick up a shawarma-filled flatbread from Ranoush Juice at number 43; or stop for kofte (and perhaps a few moments with a hookah pipe) at Abu Ali at 136 George Street, just off Edgware Road.

● After the bus passes Oxford Circus tube, get off at the **Wardour Street** stop. Cross the road, bear left and walk straight down Wardour Street – itself a centre of immigration in the 1950s, when Italians

rabic food store
n Edgware Road

and Greeks set up the cafés and coffee bars here, and in the surrounding streets. Cross Shaftesbury Avenue and you will find yourself in **Chinatown** – which has existed here in central London since the 1970s. London's traditional Chinese district is Limehouse in the east but, after much of the area was destroyed in World War II, many of the city's Chinese community decided to relocate here to join the large numbers of newly arrived immigrants from Hong Kong. Continue walking down Wardour Street and turn left into Gerrard Street, which is Chinatown's main thoroughfare. You will see restaurants – there are more than 80 within half a kilometre of here – Oriental supermarkets and businesses, and hear Cantonese spoken all around you. The best dim sum experience is to be found at New World at 1 Gerrard Place (turn left at the far end of Gerrard Street), where dishes are brought to you on a trolley. If you want a bigger meal, New Fook Lam Moon at number 10 serves some of the district's best Cantonese and Malaysian cuisine.

● Walk along Gerrard Street, turn left up Gerrard Place and recross Shaftesbury Avenue. Bear right and catch the eastbound **38** from the **Gerrard Place/ Chinatown** stop. This bus takes you through Clerkenwell and Islington to the cultural crossroads of **Dalston**, where you should get off at the **Dalston Junction Station** stop, continue up to the junction and turn left up Kingsland Road. **Ridley Road Market**, which begins opposite Dalston Kingsland overground station, is a microcosm of the diverse communities that live here. There are stalls serving Caribbean and African customers with yams and breadfruit, tilapia and snapper; and at the back of the market, Turkish and Kurdish traders hawk vegetables, fish and grisly-looking cuts of meat.

● Walk through the market and turn left up St Mark's Rise, then cross the road and catch the eastbound **236** from the **Ridley Road Market** stop to **Hackney Town Hall**. As the bus turns up **Mare Street**, you'll start to see Vietnamese cafés, restaurants and other businesses on both sides of the road. The Vietnamese community started settling in the area from 1975 – after the end of the Vietnam War – and are a small but significant presence in this part of east London. For excellent Vietnamese food along the bus route, including some wonderful stews and sturdy soups, stop off at Tre Viet at 247 Mare Street.

● Catch the northbound **106** from the **Hackney Town Hall** bus stop, and head along Clapton Road – lined with Turkish and African businesses – to **Stoke**

rrard Street, Chinatown

Newington. Get off the bus at the **Stoke Newington High Street/Brooke Road** stop and continue up to Stoke Newington High Street; home to one of the biggest Turkish communities in the UK. The businesses – from wedding shops, patisseries and supermarkets to social clubs and, of course, restaurants – that line the lower part of the high street were first established in the 1970s, when immigrants from Turkey's rural regions arrived in London to work in restaurants established by Turkish Cypriots several years earlier. One of the area's best *ocakbasis* (inexpensive grill houses specialising in deliciously tender meat) is 19 Numara Bos Cirrik II at 194 Stoke Newington High Street; Testi, a fair walk down the road at number 38, is also superb.

● Turn right along Stoke Newington High Street, then left up Stoke Newington Church Street. Walk the length of this road – which is considerably more gentrified than the high street – and, immediately after passing Clissold Park, turn right. Cross the road and catch the northbound **141** from the **Green Lanes/Stoke Newington Church Street** stop. The bus heads up **Green Lanes**, which is home to two separate Cypriot communities. The southern section up to Turnpike Lane tube is where most of the UK's Turkish Cypriots have settled. There are as many signs in Turkish here as in English. And, as in Stoke Newington, there's great eating to be had – check out Hala at 29 Grand Parade on Green Lanes, where the house speciality of beef-filled *manti* is prepared by two women sitting in the front window.

● Get off the bus at **Wood Green Station** and catch the northbound **329** from the same stop. This heads up the northern section of Green Lanes, where you will see the Greek alphabet taking over from Turkish Latin and Cyrillic characters on the signs. It was around here and **Palmers Green** – known locally as Palmers Greek – that Greek Cypriots began to settle in London from the 1930s onwards, after Cyprus was made a British colony. Palmers Green, just beyond the North Circular road, is home to the largest community of Greek Cypriots outside Cyprus. Finish your journey here by getting off the bus at **Palmers Green/ The Triangle** and turning left up Aldermans Hill to the overground station. If you're hungry, head to local favourite Babinondas, a little further up Green Lanes at number 598, for meze and a fabulous selection of Greek and Cypriot dishes.

To download this journey to your Smartphone, scan the QR code (right)

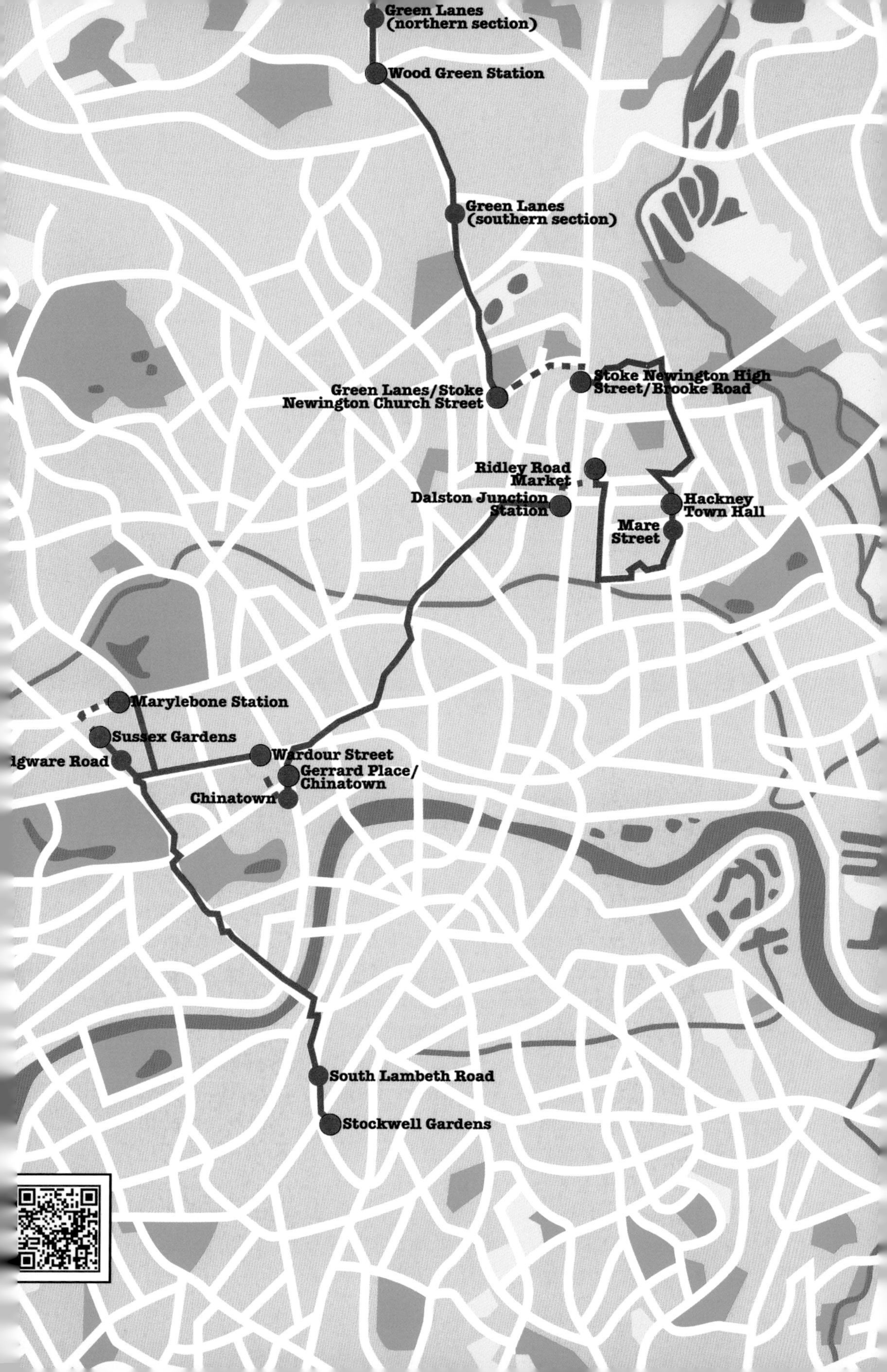
Green Lanes
(northern section)
Wood Green Station
Green Lanes
(southern section)
Green Lanes/Stoke
Newington Church Street
Stoke Newington High
Street/Brooke Road
Ridley Road
Market
Dalston Junction
Station
Hackney
Town Hall
Mare
Street
Marylebone Station
Sussex Gardens
lgware Road
Wardour Street
Gerrard Place/
Chinatown
Chinatown
South Lambeth Road
Stockwell Gardens

8. heaven on earth

Once it was simple; London, like all of England, was staunchly Catholic. Then King Henry VIII's loins stirred when Anne Boleyn walked past one day, and he realised that breaking with Rome would give him the divorce he craved. Protestantism – or the Anglican Church, with the monarch rather than the Pope at its head – came in, Catholics spent the next few centuries being persecuted and every other religion was regarded as sheer heresy. Luckily, the last 300 years or so has seen London become a much more tolerant place, in which all sects are accepted – and practise their faith openly and with the full blessing of the British government. Being the capital, London takes the lead in almost every area of religion in the UK. And the churches, mosques, synagogues and other buildings created for the city's worshippers are a glorious reflection of that spiritual eminence.

Start point: Wembley Park tube
End point: St Paul's tube
Duration: 5 hours

● Come out of **Wembley Park tube,** cross Bridge Road and turn right. Catch the southbound **206** from the **Wembley Park Station** stop and get off at **Swaminarayan Temple.** You will find yourself right outside the stunning **Shri Swaminarayan Mandir** (better known as Neasden Temple), which was built in the 1990s as a focal point for northwest London's Hindu communities. Constructed from nearly 5,000 tonnes of limestone and marble, and created in India by a huge team of craftsmen, the building was then shipped to the UK in pieces. It is the largest Hindu temple outside India. To visit its sumptuous interior, which includes seven separate shrines as well as an adjoining cultural centre and exhibition space, you need to enquire at the reception desk inside the main entrance. But – be warned – though the temple claims to be open 365 days a year, you may arrive (as this writer did) to find all gates securely closed and no sign of anyone to admit you.

● Cross the road and catch the southbound **206** or **224** from the **Swaminarayan Temple** stop down to **Knatchbull Road.** Walk back up to the junction, cross the main road and turn right to catch the eastbound **18** from the identically named **Knatchbull Road** stop on the A404. After the bus passes alongside the Westway – a raised section of motorway that leads into central London – get off at the **Edgware Road Station/Bakerloo Line** bus stop.

● Walk back and turn left down Edgware Road (going under the bridge) then, after a few minutes, turn left into Old Marylebone Road. Cross over so that you're on the same side as St Mark's Church and walk along to the **Edgware Road** stop. Catch the westbound **27** and take it to the **Queensway** stop. Once you've disembarked, continue walking down the road then turn left into Queensway. After five minutes or so, turn right into Moscow Road and walk along to **St Sophia's Greek Orthodox Cathedral.** This domed building – constructed in the late 1870s to serve Bayswater's prosperous Greek community – may look magnificent from the outside, but its interiors are truly lovely. Décor is sumptuous and lavish, with gilded frescoes and saintly mosaics featuring prominently. As the Greek government spent World War II in exile in London, St Sophia's became the de facto centre of the Greek Orthodox Church and it remains hugely significant to Hellenic Christians today.

● Once you leave the cathedral, head straight down St Petersburgh Place (situated directly opposite the main entrance), where two glorious Victorian religious centres eye each other across this quiet, leafy road. On the right is **St Matthew's Church**, built in a Gothic Revival style in 1882 and displaying some wonderful stone carvings on its exterior; on the left is the Grade I-listed **New West End Synagogue**, which dates from 1879. One of the oldest synagogues still in use in the UK, it has been described by English Heritage as 'the architectural high watermark of Anglo-Jewish architecture' – and its interior, which incorporates a beautiful raised Torah ark, is simply gorgeous.

● From St Petersburgh Place, turn left into Orme Lane – which runs alongside the synagogue – then turn right down Orme Court. Turn right at the bottom and catch the eastbound **148** from the **Orme Square** stop. This bus rounds Kensington Gardens and Hyde Park, and heads across the back of Buckingham Palace Gardens. Just after it passes Victoria Station, look right to see the Neo Byzantine **Westminster Cathedral**, which is the centre of English and Welsh Catholicism. The cathedral – which contains a glorious set of Arts & Crafts-style mosaics, as well as some wonderful gilded ceilings – was built in 1885, just over 50 years after the Roman Catholic Church was officially restored to the country three centuries after King Henry VIII and the architects of the Reformation, Thomas Cromwell and Thomas Cranmer, split from Rome and established the Church of England with the monarch as its spiritual leader. The cathedral is home to the Archbishop of Westminster, who oversees Catholicism in all London boroughs north of the River Thames, as well as several surrounding counties.

● At the entrance to Parliament Square, look first to the left for the **Methodist Central Hall** – built in a French Renaissance style at the beginning of the 20th century to commemorate the centenary of the Christian movement's founder John Wesley's death. Lovely though this building is, it is overshadowed – literally and metaphorically – by its 13th-century neighbour **Westminster Abbey**, one of the two major Anglican seats of worship in the capital. Unlike almost every other church in England, it

Shri Swaminarayan
Mandir, Neasden

holds the status of Royal Peculiar and is overseen directly by the monarch rather than a bishop. This unusual position in church hierarchy is a direct result of King Henry VIII being unwilling to dissolve the abbey in Tudor times as it contained the tombs of his father and other descendants. It continues to serve as the place in which British kings and queens are crowned; and, most recently, it was the wedding venue for Prince William and Kate Middleton.

● After crossing Westminster Bridge and passing Lambeth North tube, the bus goes along the back of the Roman Catholic **St George's Cathedral Southwark** – seat of the Archbishop of Southwark, who oversees Catholicism in Kent and all London boroughs south of the River Thames. Get off at the **Elephant & Castle Station** stop, which is situated opposite the impressive **Metropolitan Tabernacle,** centre for the capital's Reformed Baptists since 1861 and once the largest non-conformist church in the world.

● Cross the road and catch the northbound **40** from the **Elephant & Castle** stop right outside the tabernacle and take the bus up over London Bridge. Look left just before crossing the river and you will see **Southwark Cathedral** (parts of which date back to the 13th century), the Anglican mother church of Southwark Diocese, which includes pretty much all London boroughs south of the River Thames, plus parts of Surrey.

● Get off the bus at the **St Botolph Street** stop and walk back across Houndsditch before turning right up Duke's Place. Walk on for a couple of minutes then look left for **Bevis Marks Synagogue,** the oldest synagogue in the UK, which was built by London's Sephardic Jewish community in 1701 – less than 50 years after Oliver Cromwell lifted the ban on Jewish worship in England. A slightly austere building typical of the period, it occupies a somewhat discreet, tucked-away position for a religious centre of its stature. Judaism may have been allowed back into the country 350 years after it was expelled from the kingdom in the 13th century, but Cromwell expected the Jews to know their place. All synagogues, he dictated, had to be built away from main roads. This didn't affect Bevis Marks' influence. It has been the spiritual and administrative heart of Judaism in the English-speaking world for centuries.

● Retrace your steps to the **St Botolph Street** stop and catch the eastbound **254**. This bus takes you out of the old

New West End
Synagogue, Bayswater

City of London and into Whitechapel. Though the district was known for being a Jewish enclave as late as the early 20th century, it is now home to a huge Bangladeshi population. The dominant religion here is Sunni Islam and the enormous **East London Mosque**, which you can see on the right, can hold around 5,000 devotees. Built in 1985 as a focal point for the Bengali community in the borough of Tower Hamlets, it continues to expand. The London Muslim Centre, which provides facilities for the community and local businesses, opened in 2004.

● Get off the bus at **The East London Mosque** stop, then cross the road and catch the westbound **205** from the identically named stop on the other side. After passing through the City, disembark at the **Old Street Station** stop and walk back down City Road to **Wesley's Chapel** – a Grade I-listed Georgian building that was built by Methodism's founding father John Wesley in the late 1770s. Still an operational chapel with daily services, the building is also home to the Museum of Methodism. Just across the road lies **Bunhill Fields** – London's largest non-conformist cemetery from the 1600s until Victorian times – where poet William Blake is buried. It reveals much about the attitude of London's authorities to outsider religions that both this graveyard and Wesley's Chapel are situated on the fringes of the City – well beyond the old walls and as far out of sight of the populace as possible.

● Walk up to Old Street roundabout and turn left down Old Street. Walk along for a few minutes then turn right up Goswell Road. Catch the southbound **4** or **56** from the **Clerkenwell Road** stop, and take the bus down to the **St Paul's Cathedral** stop. It's a cliché to describe **St Paul's Cathedral** – London's other major seat of Anglican worship, rebuilt after the Great Fire of London in 1666 destroyed most of the ancient City – as Sir Christopher Wren's masterpiece. But it is. The sheer scale of the building, which is covered in intricate carvings from both the celestial and natural worlds, was no doubt enough to remind 17th-century Londoners of the power of God alone. But the beauty of its Neoclassical architecture and the purity of colour in its stonework take it to another level altogether. Take time to explore it properly. Aesthetically at least, it's the absolute pinnacle of London's rich religious world.

To download this journey to your Smartphone, scan the QR code (right).

Wembley Park Station
Swaminarayan Temple
Knatchbull Road
Knatchbull Road
Edgware Road/
Bakerloo Line
Edgware Road
Queensway
St Sophia's Greek
Orthodox Cathedral
St Matthew's Church
New West End
Synagogue
Orme Square
Methodist
Central Hall
Westminster
Abbey
Westminster Cathedral
St George's
Cathedral
Southwark
Metropolitan Tabernacle
Elephant &
Castle Station
Southwark Cathedral
St Paul's Cathedral
Clerkenwell Road
Old Street Station
Wesley's Chapel
The East
London Mosque
St Botolph Street
Bevis Marks
Synagogue

9. build it up

As the capital city and, for so long, the centre of the British Empire, London has always represented something of a showcase for ambitious architects. Renzo Piano's Shard, the 309-metre elongated pyramid that dominates the South Bank, is just the latest iconic structure to be added to the London skyline. And modern visionaries such as he, Norman Foster – responsible for the Gherkin – and Lloyd's Building architect Richard Rogers continue the forward-thinking attitude to city-shaping displayed by predecessors Christopher Wren, Nicholas Hawksmoor and George Gilbert Scott. London is the beneficiary. Almost every design style of the past 600 years is on show here; and, as a result, the city has become an ever-changing architectural masterpiece.

Start point: Holland Park tube
End point: Canary Wharf DLR
Duration: 6 hours

● Exit **Holland Park tube** and turn right, then take the first left down Holland Park. Walk straight down here onto Abbotsbury Road, then continue alongside the park until you reach the junction with Melbury Road. Turn left here and look out for **The Tower House** at number 29. Built as the home of architect William Burges in 1876, this superb example of Victorian Gothic Revival architecture draws as heavily on fairytale as it does medieval design traditions. Burges was, after all, closely linked with the Pre-Raphaelite artists of the time. He died here in 1881.

● Continue to the bottom of Melbury Road then turn left and catch the eastbound **9** or **10** from the **Kensington High Street/Earls Court Road** stop. Just after the bus passes High Street Kensington tube, it heads along the front of the former **Barkers** and **Derry & Toms** department stores. Built between the 1930s and 1950s, this seven-storey Art Deco complex is now a shopping centre. Look up to see stunning bas-relief friezes of tradesmen at work.

● As the bus goes along Hyde Park, look left for the **Albert Memorial** – another glorious piece of Gothic Revival design, commissioned by Queen Victoria after the death of her husband Prince Albert. The work of George Gilbert Scott, the memorial is surrounded by Neoclassical statues representing the arts and sciences, and the continents of the world.

● Get off the bus at the **Royal Albert Hall** stop and continue down Kensington Gore, passing **Lowther Lodge** on the right. This Queen Anne Style building, home to the Royal Geographic Society since 1912, was designed in the mid-1870s by Richard Norman Shaw. Though its statues of the great British explorers inevitably steal the show, the sunflowers on the chimney stacks are equally worthy of note, and are stylistic motifs that also appear in Arts & Crafts designs of the period.

● Turn right down Exhibition Road, then right again into Prince Consort Road and walk past the back of the High Victorian **Royal Albert Hall**. As you continue down the road, you will also pass Sir Aston Webb's Neoclassical **Royal School of Mines** (now part of Imperial College) and Sir Arthur Blomfield's Flemish Mannerist **Royal College of Music** on the left.

● Catch the southbound **360** from the **Prince Consort Road** stop. As it starts heading through the district known informally as Albertopolis, look first to the left for Webb's Medieval-cum-Renaissance façade to the **Victoria & Albert Museum** before turning to the right to see Alfred Waterhouse's terracotta-clad **Natural History Museum.** Built in a loose Romanesque style between 1873 and 1880, the building – which features thousands of beautiful and intricate animal, bird and insect carvings – conveys a gothic, almost cathedral-like feel. Just after the bus passes South Kensington tube, it heads down Fulham Road, and passes the **Bibendum** restaurant on the right. Situated in Michelin House (Bibendum is the official name of the Michelin Man), the restaurant is surrounded by some of the finest Art Nouveau architecture in the UK. Designed by Michelin's in-house architect François Espinasse in 1911, the building features stained-glass windows based on the French tyre company's advertisements, as well as exterior tiles decorated with maps and motor-racing scenes. The bus then continues down to the north bank of the Thames, providing you with a wonderful view of Art Deco icon **Battersea Power Station** – the largest brick-built building in Europe.

● Get off the 360 at the **Pimlico Station** stop and continue walking along Bessborough Street and Drummond Gate before crossing Vauxhall Bridge Road, turning right and following signs to Millbank – the road that runs parallel to the river. Turn left onto Millbank and take the northbound **87** from the **Vauxhall Bridge Road** stop. As the bus makes its way up to Parliament Square, it passes the odd couple of the **Tate Britain** and **Millbank Tower** – Neoclassical and Brutalist neighbours that provide one of London's most striking contrasts.

● Though the **Houses of Parliament** – designed by Charles Barry in 1834 after fire destroyed most of the 11th-century Palace of Westminster – are mock-Gothic, **Westminster Abbey,** on the other side of the road as you enter Parliament Square, is the real deal. Work was begun on the current building in 1245, when King Henry II selected the church that originally stood here as his burial site. It has served as the place in which British monarchs are crowned and interred ever since.

● Get off the bus at the **Parliament Square** stop on Whitehall, and catch the northbound **12** from the same place. This immediately takes you past the Italianate **Foreign & Commonwealth Office** on your left, before heading up Whitehall to pass Inigo Jones' Palladian **Banqueting House** – the first Neoclassical building to be

Bibendum, Fulham Road

constructed in England – on the right. The bus then heads up the elegant curve of **Regent Street** – the work of King George IV's favourite architect John Nash – before terminating at the **Margaret Street/Oxford Circus stop**.

● Walk back down Regent Street, turn left into Great Castle Street and then right down Great Portland Street. Cross Oxford Street, bear right and walk down Argyll Street to the **Liberty** department store. Built in a striking Tudorbethan style by Edwin T Hall in 1924, this famous building was constructed using timbers from two British battleships.

● Retrace your steps to Oxford Street, then turn right and catch the eastbound **25** from the **Great Titchfield Street** stop. As the bus makes its way along the road, look to the right for Robert Lutyens' Art Deco **Pantheon** (now occupied by Marks & Spencer). The far end of Oxford Street is dominated by the Brutalist **Centre Point**, which towers above Tottenham Court Road tube. Loved and loathed in equal measure by Londoners, this 34-storey building was constructed between 1963 and 1966, and is now Grade II-listed.

● When the bus turns up Bloomsbury Way, look left for the Neoclassical **St George's Bloomsbury** church. Built in the early Georgian period by master architect Nicholas Hawksmoor, who based his design on Middle Eastern temples, it takes the classical theme and runs with it – there's even a statue of George I in Roman dress on top of its pyramid steeple. William Hogarth saw fit to include this brilliantly over-the-top creation in the background of his infamous 'Gin Lane' print of 1751.

● Get off the bus at the **Chancery Lane Station** stop – looking out for the original Elizabethan shop fronts on the opposite side of the road, which form the façade of **Staple Inn** (the oldest of the surviving Inns of Court) – then walk back up High Holborn and turn left down Chancery Lane. Pass James Pennethorne's Gothic Revival **Maughan Library** before emerging onto Fleet Street, opposite the **Inner Temple Gateway** – a 17th-century reproduction of the gate that stood there from the 1100s onwards. Turn left down Fleet Street and walk past Sir Christopher Wren's **St Bride's Church** (the steeple of which is the inspiration for the tiered wedding cake) on the right and, on the left at number 120, Sir Owen Williams' black-and-chrome Art Deco **Daily Express Building**.

● Take the westbound **11, 15** or **23** from the **Shoe Lane** stop on the St Bride

The Shard, London Bridge

Church side of Fleet Street. All buses pass the Art Deco **Savoy Hotel** on the left as they make their way along the Strand to the **Bedford Street** stop, where you need to disembark. From here, continue walking along the Strand and turn right up Bedford Street. Turn right into Henrietta Street and emerge into **Covent Garden** piazza, home to Inigo Jones' Italianate porticoed square and Renaissance-style St Paul's church.

● Walk right through Covent Garden market to emerge at the Royal Opera House end of the piazza. Continue straight ahead down Russell Street. Turn right down Catherine Street and catch the southbound **RV1** from the **Covent Garden/Catherine Street** stop. This bus first takes you past Sir William Chambers' Neoclassical **Somerset House** before driving alongside the iconic **London Eye**, built as part of the city's Millennium celebrations. Next up are the Brutalist South Bank buildings – the **Royal Festival Hall**, the **Queen Elizabeth Hall**, the **Hayward Gallery** and the **National Theatre** – which were constructed in the early 1950s to create a new entertainment sector on the neglected south side of the Thames. The bus continues around the back of Bankside, providing excellent views of the Art Deco **Oxo Tower**, whose architects got around advertising restrictions by incorporating the stock-cube company's name into its window designs, and the **Tate Modern** gallery – which occupies the former Bankside Power Station, designed by Giles Gilbert Scott in 1947.

● When the RV1 starts to cross the Gothic Revival **Tower Bridge**, look to the left for a great view of Sir Norman Foster's headlamp-like **City Hall** and Renzo Piano's **The Shard**, which is the UK's tallest occupied building (only Yorkshire's Emley Moor transmitting station is higher). The bridge also affords a wonderful sight of the London skyline, and Foster's sustainable **30 St Mary Axe** (known affectionately as 'the Gherkin'), **Tower 42** – the Postmodern skyscraper better known by its old name The Natwest Tower – and Wren's 17th-century masterpiece, **St Paul's Cathedral**, are all clearly visible. Get off the bus at the **Tower of London** stop.

● As you walk up Tower Bridge Road and turn left onto Tower Hill, you will see the **Tower of London** to your left. A riot of architectural design, the complex was begun with the Norman **White Tower** in 1078 and was expanded in the 12th and 13th centuries in a range of medieval styles. Catch the westbound **15** from **The Tower of London** stop, which takes you

ne Tudor gatehouse at St
artholomew the Great, Smithfield

past Wren's **Monument** – a 60m Doric column that commemorates the Great Fire of London in 1666 – and the Neoclassical grandeur of his **St Paul's Cathedral.**

● Get off the bus at the **City Thameslink/ Ludgate Circus** stop, walk back towards St Paul's and turn left up Old Bailey. Cross over Newgate Street and continue up Giltspur Street until you emerge in Smithfield – home to the **Tudor gatehouse of St Bartholomew the Great** (straight ahead from Giltspur Street) and Sir Horace Jones' stunning cast-iron **Smithfield Market** building. Walk through the market and turn right onto Charterhouse Street. At the end of this road lies Charterhouse Square, the north side of which is occupied by the **London Charterhouse,** a former priory that is now a complex of medieval residences, some of which date back to the 14th century. The Charterhouse is private property, but viewings can be arranged at www.thecharterhouse.org. At the southeast of the square, the Brutalist towerblocks of the **Barbican Estate** – built in the 1960s and 1970s to rejuvenate the bomb-shattered Cripplegate district – can be seen towering over this peaceful enclave on the edge of the City.

● Return to Smithfield, turn right into the alleyway between the gatehouse of St Bartholomew the Great and St Bartholomew's Hospital, and walk along Little Britain. When you reach the junction, turn left onto Montague Street and catch the eastbound **100** from the **Little Britain** stop. As this heads along London Wall, look out for the Neoclassical **All Hallows on the Wall** church, designed by George Dance the Younger in 1767, on the left. Get off the bus at the **Houndsditch** stop.

● Catch the eastbound **135** from the same stop all the way out to **Canary Wharf Station. One Canada Square,** the Postmodern pyramid-topped tower that dominates this futuristic huddle of buildings was designed by Cesar Pelli in 1988, and was the first marker to be put down in this mini Manhattan out in London's Docklands. A brash symbol of 1980s affluence that broke tradition by setting up shop away from the City, it is something of an extended middle finger to London's traditional financial centre upriver. This upstart, though, has now become iconic an its futuristic design now seems almost quaint. Glitzy and gleaming it may be, bu like all the other buildings in this journey, i now merely part of the fabric of the city.

To download this journey to your Smartphone, scan the QR code (right)

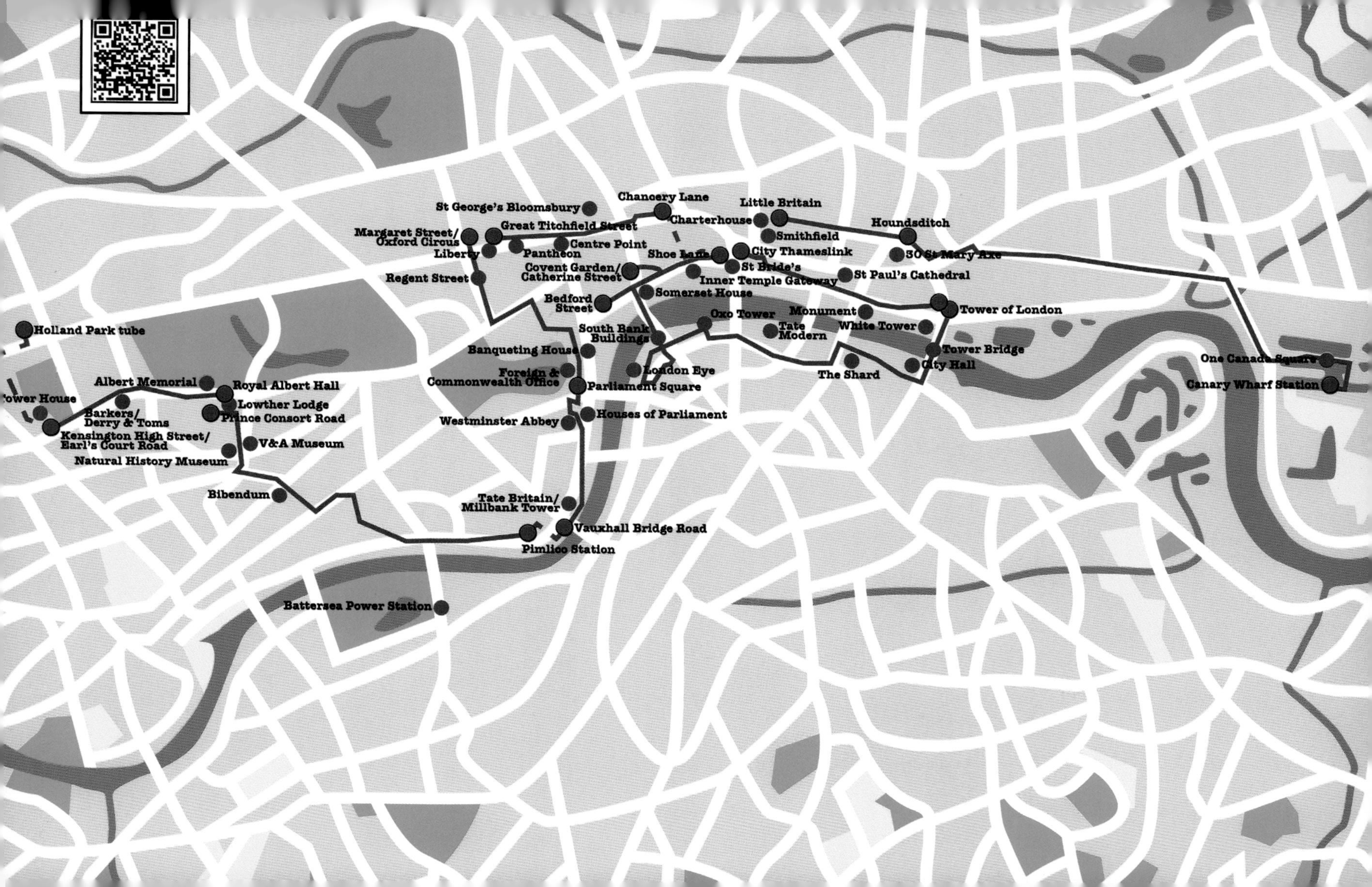
Holland Park tube
Albert Memorial
Royal Albert Hall
Lowther Lodge
Prince Consort Road
Barkers/
Derry & Toms
Kensington High Street/
Earl's Court Road
V&A Museum
Natural History Museum
Bibendum
St George's Bloomsbury
Chancery Lane
Margaret Street/
Oxford Circus
Great Titchfield Street
Charterhouse
Little Britain
Houndsditch
Liberty
Pantheon
Centre Point
Smithfield
Shoe Lane
City Thameslink
30 St Mary Axe
Regent Street
Covent Garden/
Catherine Street
St Bride's
Inner Temple Gateway
St Paul's Cathedral
Bedford
Street
Somerset House
Oxo Tower
Monument
Tower of London
South Bank
Buildings
Tate
Modern
White Tower
Banqueting House
Tower Bridge
Foreign &
Commonwealth Office
London Eye
City Hall
The Shard
One Canada Square
Canary Wharf Station
Parliament Square
Houses of Parliament
Westminster Abbey
Tate Britain/
Millbank Tower
Vauxhall Bridge Road
Pimlico Station
Battersea Power Station

10. royal london

Ever since King Edward the Confessor rebuilt Westminster Abbey as his burial place in the early 11th century, London has been synonymous with royalty. William the Conqueror, fresh from the Battle of Hastings, established his base here in 1066 – building the first parts of the Tower of London – and his descendants, which include such legendary monarchs as Henry VIII, Elizabeth I, Charles II, George IV, Victoria and current Queen Elizabeth II – have all made the city their home. Palaces and parklands built for royal pleasure can be seen throughout central London, and almost every street in Zone One boasts some regal connection. Royalty may not have the political power it once did, but – as the Queen's recent diamond jubilee celebrations showed – it is still capable of captivating and influencing British society as much as it ever did.

Start point: Paddington tube
End point: Green Park tube
Duration: 5 hours

● Come out of **Paddington tube** (the District Line branch) and turn right. Walk straight ahead along Praed Street to **St Mary's Hospital**, which was the birthplace – in 1982 and 1984 respectively – of Princes William and Harry; the sons of Prince Charles and Princess Diana, who are currently second and third in line to the British throne. Princess Anne, daughter of Queen Elizabeth II, also chose to have her children here – Peter and Zara Phillips were born in the maternity wing in 1977 and 1981.

● Turn around and walk back up Praed Street, then catch the westbound **27** from the **Paddington Station** stop, on the opposite side of the road to the Hilton London Paddington Hotel. The bus passes through the Royal Borough of Kensington & Chelsea – which, as it was the birthplace of Queen Victoria, was granted its title upon her death in 1901 – and heads down Kensington Church Street. Get off at the **York House Place/Kensington High Street** stop, continue down the road and then turn right into York House Place. This road turns into the alley-like York Passage, which leads you to the edge of Kensington Gardens. Upon entering the park, you'll see **Kensington Palace** to your left. As well as being the current home of the Duke and Duchess of Cambridge – William and Kate to casual royal-watchers – it was the official home of Diana, Princess of Wales, from 1981 until her death in 1997. Other previous incumbents have included William of Orange, Queen Anne, and Georges I and II. Queen Victoria – whose gleaming marble statue sits in front of the palace's eastern façade – was born here in 1819.

● Walk along the front of the palace and turn right down the Broad Walk path. Follow this all the way down to the southern edge of Kensington Gardens and, upon emerging from the park, turn right and catch the eastbound **9** from the **Palace Gate** stop. Look to the left for Sir George Gilbert Scott's **Albert Memorial** – erected in 1872 to commemorate Queen Victoria's late husband Prince Albert, who died of typhoid in 1861.

● After passing Hyde Park Corner, the bus heads up Piccadilly and past **Green Park** on the right. Unlike all of London's other royal parks, there are no formal flowerbeds in this green space. The reason for this, apparently, is that Catherine of Braganza, wife of King Charles II (who built the park in the 1660s, as he wanted to be able to walk from Buckingham Palace to the northwest corner of Kensington Gardens without having to leave royal parkland), discovered the famously unfaithful monarch had been picking flowers from here and presenting them to his mistresses. She then ordered that all existing flowers be uprooted and forbade the planting of any more. Unfortunately for the queen, a lack of easily reachable foliage did little to stop Charles' infidelities.

● When the bus turns off Piccadilly into St James's Street, look straight ahead for **St James's Palace**, the administrative centre of the British monarchy. Built in the 1530s by King Henry VIII, the palace was – until recently – the official residence of Prince Charles. It is now home to Princess Anne and Princess Beatrice of York. Charles now lives at **Clarence House**, the former home of Queen Elizabeth the Queen Mother, between the walls of St James's Palace and the Mall behind. The bus continues along **Pall Mall,** the southern side of which nearly all belongs to the royal family's Crown Estate. As late as 1960, the one exception was number 79 – which was granted by King Charles II to royal mistress Nell Gwyn.

● After leaving Pall Mall, the 9 heads down **Cockspur Street**, where a statue of King George III (subject of the film *The Madness of King George*) on horseback has stood since 1836. After going through Trafalgar Square, it passes another equestrian statue on the right at the top of **Whitehall** – this time of King Charles I, who was executed near here in 1649. Charles is situated on the spot where King Edward I erected the last of the 12 crosses to mark the funeral route of his wife Eleanor of Castile in 1294. The original cross was destroyed in the Civil War, but a replica stands in the forecourt of **Charing Cross Station**, which you pass almost immediately on the right.

● Get off the bus at the **Aldwych/Drury Lane** stop and walk back down Aldwych. Turn right into Catherine Street. The **Theatre Royal Drury Lane**, which has its main entrance at the top of this road, has as many royal connections as its title would suggest. It was here, in 1668, that Charles II met his most famous lover Nell Gwyn, an actress who had worked her

St James's Palace

way up from mere orange-seller; and, not to be outdone by his ancestor, the Prince Regent (later George IV) first set eyes on actress Mary Robinson here in 1779. She went on to become his mistress for the next two years, before being unceremoniously – and very publicly – dumped.

● Catch the eastbound **RV1** from the **Covent Garden/Catherine Street** stop, which takes you past **Somerset House** – once the residence of Queen Elizabeth I, James I, Charles I and Charles II before it was extensively renovated by Sir Christopher Wren in the late 17th century – and over the Thames into Southwark. After the bus recrosses the river at Tower Bridge, get off at the **Tower of London** stop. This famous castle, which you can see to the left, has seen more than 1,000 years of royal history. William the Conqueror built the **White Tower** here in 1078 and the fortifications were expanded and developed by later medieval monarchs. It was here that 12-year-old King Edward V and his 10-year-old brother – the 'princes in the tower' – disappeared in 1483, conveniently leaving the throne to their uncle Richard III; and where Anne Boleyn, second wife of Henry VIII, was beheaded by sword in 1536. In 1554, Anne's daughter, Queen Elizabeth I, was imprisoned here by her half-sister Mary before she ascended to the throne.

● Walk around the castle onto Tower Hill, passing all the open-top tourist bus stops, and catch the westbound **15** from **The Tower of London** stop. The bus takes you past **St Paul's Cathedral**, where Prince Charles and Lady Diana Spencer were married in 1981, and along Fleet Street. Look to the right immediately after the Dundee Courier building at number 186, and you will see a statue of Queen Elizabeth I set high into the wall of **St Dunstan in the West** church. This 1586 effigy – the only existing one made of the queen in her lifetime – was originally part of the Ludgate, but was moved here in 1760 when the gate was demolished.

● Shortly after the bus passes **St Martin in the Fields** – parish church of the royal family and final resting place of Nell Gwyn – on the right, get off at the **Trafalgar Square** stop. Walk back in the direction the bus came from and turn right under Admiralty Arch. Walk straight down The Mall, the long, straight road that leads directly to **Buckingham Palace** – official London residence of the monarch since 1837. The balcony at the front of the palace is, of course,

Statue of Queen Elizabeth I at St Dunstan in the West, Fleet Street

where the royal family gather to celebrate on public occasions – most recently for the wedding of Prince William and Kate Middleton, and the Queen's diamond jubilee.

● Turn left at the palace then left again up Birdcage Walk, and stroll all the way to Parliament Square. **Westminster Abbey,** on the right-hand side of the square, was first earmarked as a royal burial church in 1042 by Edward the Confessor – who was interred here in 1066 – and notable tombs include those of Anne of Cleves, Elizabeth I, James I and Charles II. The abbey has since served as a place of coronation for every British monarch since the crownings of Harold and William the Conqueror in 1066. It has also been the scene of several royal weddings, beginning with that of Henry I and Matilda of Scotland in 1100 and ending with the 2011 nuptials of Prince William and Kate Middleton. To the left of the abbey, the **Palace of Westminster** – more commonly known as the Houses of Parliament – was the main royal residence in London until 1512. Nowadays, the monarch is forbidden from entering its principal chamber, the House of Commons; a tradition that dates back to 1642 and a raging King Charles I's attempt to force his way in to arrest anti-royalist MPs. It wasn't the last time he lost his head.

● Walk up Whitehall (the road to the left of the one on which you entered Parliament Square) and catch the northbound **3, 12, 88, 159** or **453** from the **Parliament Square** stop all the way to the **Oxford Circus Station** or **Margaret Street/Oxford Circus** stops. Just after the bus turns from Piccadilly Circus onto Regent Street, look left for a glimpse of **Chinawhite,** the upmarket nightclub that was once frequented by Prince Harry.

● Cross the road and catch the southbound **C2** from the identically named stop on the other side. This bus heads back down Regent Street before turning right down Conduit Street into Mayfair. When the road becomes **Bruton Street,** look to the left for number 17 – now a branch of Regus office solutions – which is where Queen Elizabeth II was born on 21 April, 1926. Get off the bus at the **Green Park Station** stop, continue walking along Piccadilly, then turn right up White Horse Street. End your royal journey with a well-deserved drink at the suitably named **King's Arms** in Shepherd Market.

To download this journey to your Smartphone, scan the QR code (right).

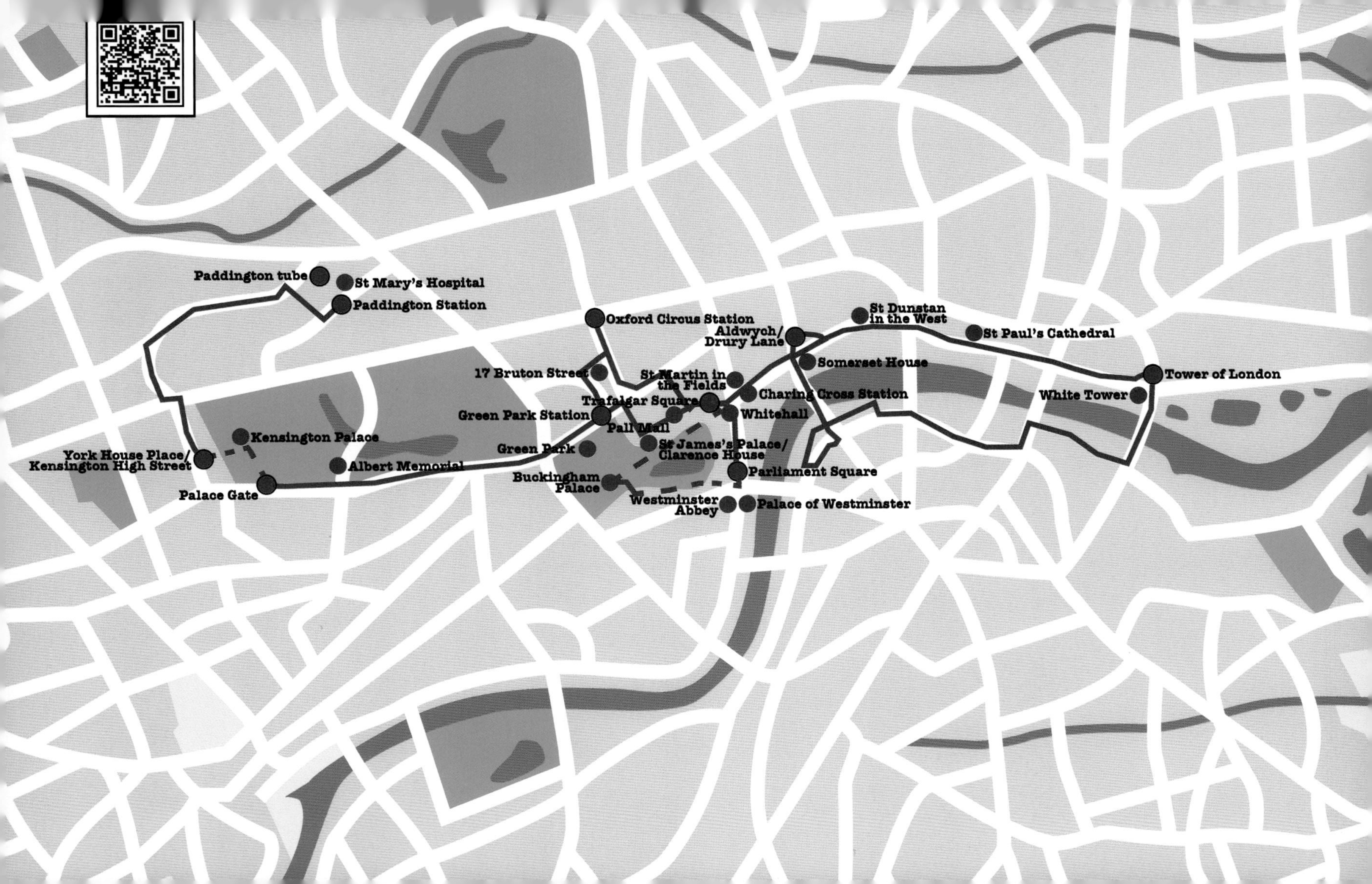
Paddington tube
St Mary's Hospital
Paddington Station
Oxford Circus Station
St Dunstan in the West
Aldwych/ Drury Lane
St Paul's Cathedral
Somerset House
17 Bruton Street
St Martin in the Fields
Tower of London
Charing Cross Station
White Tower
Trafalgar Square
Green Park Station
Whitehall
Pall Mall
Kensington Palace
Green Park
St James's Palace/ Clarence House
York House Place/ Kensington High Street
Albert Memorial
Parliament Square
Buckingham Palace
Palace Gate
Westminster Abbey
Palace of Westminster

Portobello Market, Notting Hill

11. saturday markets

Saturday is traditionally London's day of leisure. The working week is at an end and Friday-night hangovers are easing away by the time Londoners emerge into the fresh air to visit the city's weekend markets. Though shopping is on their minds – some new clothes and accessories for the big night ahead, perhaps; or a quirky antique to improve the look of the bedroom? – they come mainly to places such as Portobello, Dalston and Hackney to meet friends, browse the stalls and pick up some lunch from the many street food vendors. This journey places the emphasis on fun rather than functional, though its first stop – Billingsgate Fish Market – is included for its exciting atmosphere and sense of history. It does, however, have sole.

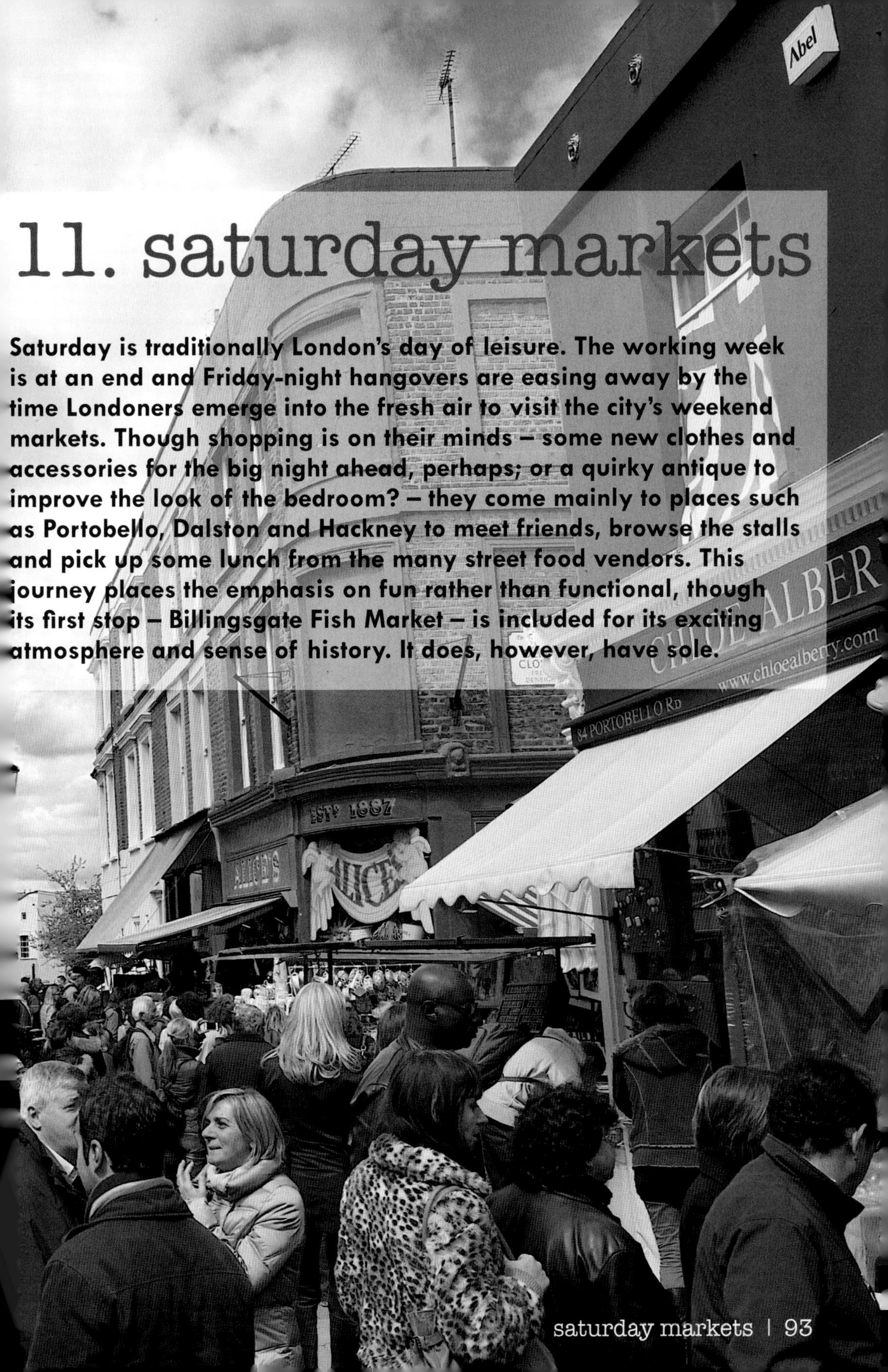

Start point: Canary Wharf DLR
End point: Ladbroke Grove tube
Duration: 4.5 hours

● Though financial centre Canary Wharf may be known for an altogether different type of market, its gleaming towers and glitzy shopping arcades provide the gateway to one of London's most ancient trading centres. **Billingsgate Fish Market** didn't always exist out here in the Docklands – its original location, from the 16th century onwards, was at Billingsgate Wharf near London Bridge – but it has occupied its current 13-acre site since 1982. Until very recently, only licensed fish porters (recognisable by their white sailcloth smocks and flat-topped hats) were permitted to move boxes of fish around the market – a law that went back to mid 1600s – but, in 2012, these restrictions were lifted, bringing an end to nearly 400 years of tradition. Many porters are still employed at the market and, other than the occasional glimpse of modernity, the scene here is still very similar to how it would have been in Tudor times.

● On Saturday mornings, Billingsgate Fish Market is open from 5am to 8.30am, and it's best to get there as early as possible – if only to see the staggering variety of fish and seafood that's quickly bought up by London's early rising food retailers. To walk there from **Canary Wharf DLR**, come out of the station via the South Colonnade exit, turn left and walk onto Trafalgar Way. Follow this road for a few minutes and you will arrive at the entrance to the market, which is situated on a small roundabout.

● Once you've had your fill of all things piscatorial, exit the market the same way you came in and cross Trafalgar Way. Catch the northbound **277** from the **Billingsgate Market** bus stop and take this all the way up to **Dalston Junction**. Get off the bus and continue walking up Dalston Lane, then turn right up Kingsland High Street. Situated opposite Dalston Kingsland overground station, the colourful **Ridley Road Market** began as a small collection of stalls in the late 19th century. Nowadays, it's a much bigger affair, and its pitches are a true reflection of the district's large Caribbean and African population. Saltfish, goat meat, mangoes and yams sit next to potatoes and peas on the displays, and cheap goods – from budget deodorant to knock-off CDs – are available wherever you turn. Though Dalston is rapidly becoming something of a Shoreditch

Broadway Market, Hackney

spillover, with artists, musicians and other hipsters moving in to take advantage of cheap rents and good nightlife, Ridley Road Market shows little sign of gentrification. It's scuzzy, smelly and a bit boisterous. And it's all the more fun for that.

● Walk all the way through Ridley Road Market and turn left up St Mark's Rise at the far end. Catch the southbound **236** from the **Ridley Road Market** stop and take the bus all the way to the **Broadway Market** stop in Hackney. **Broadway Market**, which stretches down from the acres of greenery at London Fields to the Regent's Canal, is a much more fashionable hangout – and is the epicentre of London's ultra-trendy street food scene. Though trading has taken place here for 50 years or so, it is only since the establishment of a dedicated food market in 2004 that the area's fortunes have really taken off. Nowadays, stalls selling everything from specialist Scotch eggs and homemade bread to Indian thalis and hot-pork sandwiches have been joined by pitches specialising in cutting-edge fashion, crafts and records. And, what with all the trendy boutiques and cafés that have opened up alongside, the market has become an essential Saturday experience for any East Londoner with aspirations of coolness.

● After exploring Broadway Market, return to the bus stop and continue walking up Westgate Street. At the end of the road, turn left up Mare Street, cross over the road and catch the southbound **48** from the **King Edward's Road** bus stop. The bus then travels through Hackney, Shoreditch and the City, before crossing London Bridge and terminating at **London Bridge Station**. Once you get off the bus, walk back out of the bus station and turn left down Borough High Street. There are entrances to **Borough Market** on Bedale Street and Southwark Street, both on the right. This famous food market is one of London's largest, and sells to both trade and the public. Like the much smaller Broadway Market, it's as much of a social hangout as a place to fill your shopping bag, and the cafés and pubs that surround the cast-iron market hall are every bit as popular as the stalls. Though it's these, which sell everything from artisan cheeses and homemade pies to Spanish chorizo and spiced cider, that are the real stars of the show.

● Return to Borough High Street, turn right and catch the **35, 40, 133** or

Pies at Borough Market

343 from the Southwark Street bus stop down to **Elephant & Castle/Newington Causeway.** Continue down the road and use the admittedly complicated underpass system to get to St George's Road (the second road on the right off the roundabout), then cross over and catch the westbound **148** from the **Elephant & Castle Station** bus stop all the way to **Shepherd's Bush Green.** Get off the bus and carry on walking up the road before turning left onto Uxbridge Road. **Shepherd's Bush Market,** the entrance to which is a couple of minutes further along on the left, is another local market in the Ridley Road tradition – albeit with a more Indian influence. Low prices rather than high fashion (and indeed high quality) are to be found here, and the rows of stalls that line the railway line down to Goldhawk Lane tube station specialise mainly in bargain clothes, shoes and accessories. There are plenty of food stalls, too; as well as pitches selling all the household items, cheap toys, London souvenirs and Hindi DVDs you could ever need.

● Return to the Uxbridge Road end of Shepherd's Bush Market and walk back to the **Shepherd's Bush Green** stop. Catch the eastbound **94** or **148** from here to **Notting Hill Gate Station/ Hillgate Street,** then get off the bus and bear left up Pembridge Road, following the signs – and the people – to **Portobello Market.** This world-famous market – featured in everything from 1971's *Bedknobs and Broomsticks* to the 1999 Hugh Grant and Julia Roberts film *Notting Hill* – began life as a centre of the fruit and vegetable trade in the Victorian era. The arrival of antiques dealers in the 1940s and 1950s made it a must-visit for anyone with an eye for aesthetics, and the fashion set moved in shortly afterwards to cement the market's reputation. It's now one of the best – and certainly the most interesting – places in London to pick up vintage clothes, jewellery and stylish homeware. A fascinating reflection of the district's incongruous mix of aristocratic and Caribbean residents, the market is a heady and often bewildering experience which can take dedicated Saturday shoppers several hours to work their way through. So you'll probably need a drink and a bit of a sit-down afterwards. The Castle, towards the Ladbroke Grove end of the market, is an excellent place for settling down with a pint and watching the people go by.

To download this journey to your Smartphone, scan the QR code (right)

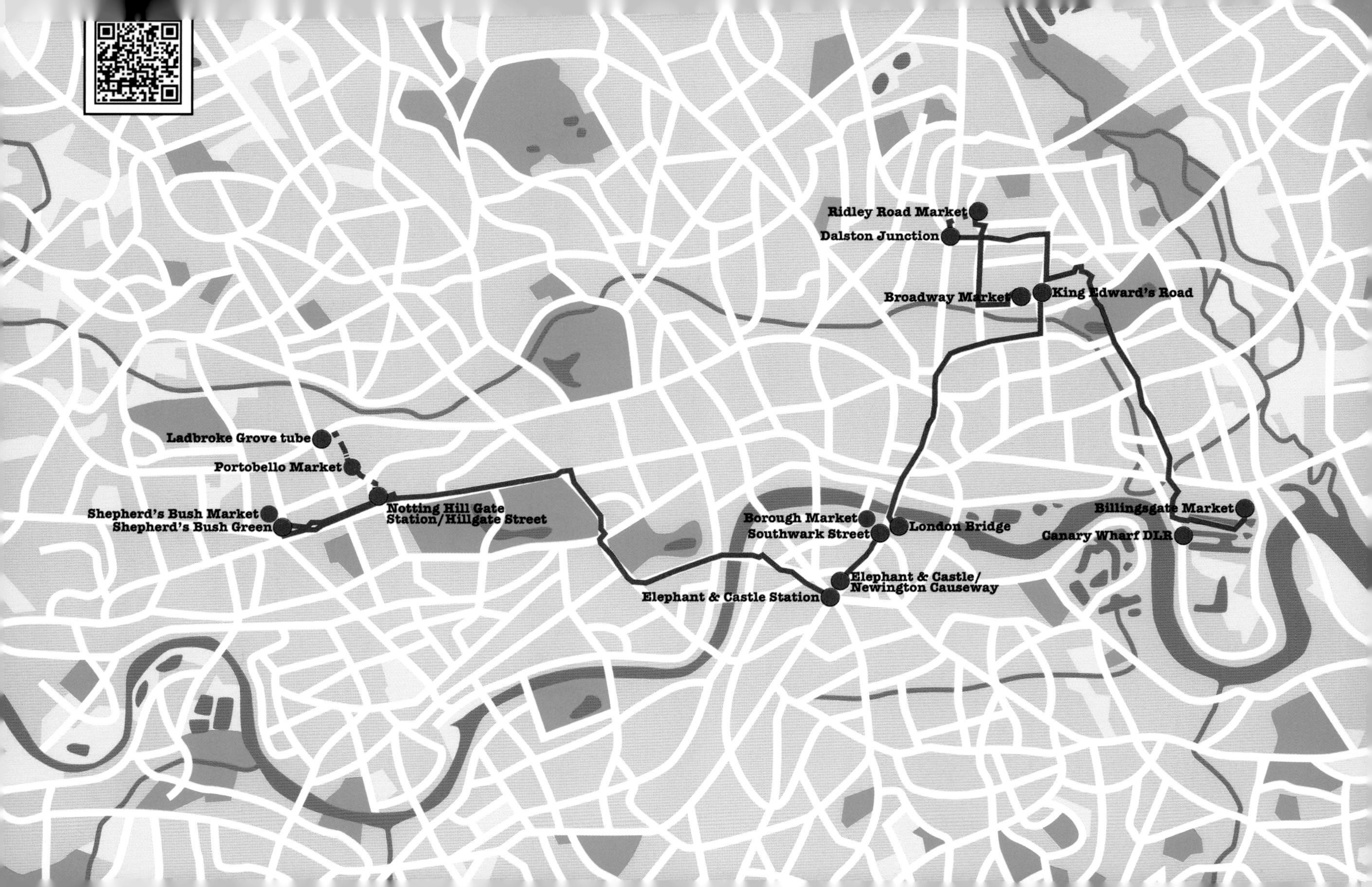
Ridley Road Market
Dalston Junction
Broadway Market
King Edward's Road
Ladbroke Grove tube
Portobello Market
Shepherd's Bush Market
Shepherd's Bush Green
Notting Hill Gate
Station/Hillgate Street
Borough Market
Southwark Street
London Bridge
Billingsgate Market
Canary Wharf DLR
Elephant & Castle/
Newington Causeway
Elephant & Castle Station

12. urban music

It's no exaggeration to say that London is one of the greatest musical cities on earth. Its buildings, streets, squares and parks have been celebrated by the capital's songsmiths for as long as there have been people living along the Thames, but it's only in the era of recorded music that these tunes have entered the national – and international – consciousness. Though many of the greatest songs to come out of London – *Itchycoo Park*, *Up the Junction*, *White Riot* or, erm, *The Wombling Song* – are about life in its suburbs, the city has produced just as many artists who have turned their attention to Zone One. This journey takes you around some of the sites and landmarks that inspired those tunes and, thanks to London being such a rich creative source for generations of songwriters, past many a street sign that will inadvertently get you whistling a familiar tune.

Start point: Warwick Avenue tube
End point: Green Park tube
Duration: 3 hours

● Leave **Warwick Avenue tube** through the Clifton Gardens exit (which is on the right just after the ticket barriers) and walk up the steps. It is beneath the entrance sign here that Welsh singer-songwriter Duffy breaks up with her lover in her 2008 hit *Warwick Avenue*. The song, unfortunately, doesn't reflect a real incident. The name of the tube station simply appealed to Duffy – who had recently relocated from Gwynedd to London – after she got off at the wrong Bakerloo Line stop.

● Walk back a few metres and turn right into Clifton Gardens, then catch the eastbound **6** from the **Warwick Avenue Station** stop. The bus passes through Maida Vale and Little Venice before going under **the Westway** – on which a couple lose their way in Blur's *For Tomorrow* – and down Edgware Road. The traffic island next to the cinema at the bottom of this road is where the **Tyburn Tree gallows** once stood, and it was around this spot that London's first commercial songwriters made their money. Ballad sellers would flock here on hanging days to hawk songsheets – often purporting to be the condemned criminal's last words – to a crowd eager for souvenirs of the execution.

● After heading along Oxford Street and down Regent Street – passing the alley on the left that leads to **Carnaby Street**, headquarters of 'the Carnebetian army' in The Kinks' *Dedicated Follower of Fashion* – the bus reaches **Piccadilly Circus**. This area makes its most famous appearance in the World War I singalong *It's a Long Way To Tipperary*, popularised when soldiers across Europe would belt out the chorus of 'Goodbye Piccadilly, farewell Leicester Square' to keep up their trench-weary spirit. Morrissey's 1990 single *Piccadilly Palare* takes a different slant – the former Smiths frontman focused on the district's 19th-century notoriety as a haunt of male prostitutes.

● Get off the bus at the **Trafalgar Square** stop, then walk back a couple of metres and catch the southbound **3** from the **Trafalgar Square/Charing Cross Station** stop. The bus goes down Whitehall and through Parliament Square before crossing Lambeth Bridge and heading along Lambeth Road. Look to the right for **Lambeth Walk** – the street once known for the Cockney street market that inspired the 1937 song *The Lambeth Walk*. This tune and the dance that accompanies it, which feature in the musical *Me And My Girl*, were so well-known in the late 1930s and early 1940s that leading German Nazis made speeches condemning its 'animalistic hopping'. British leaders were much more accepting. King George VI and Queen Elizabeth attended a performance of the song in the late 1930s, and both shouted out the 'Oi!' at the end of each chorus.

● The 3 continues through Kennington into **Brixton** – setting for The Clash's 1979 song *The Guns of Brixton*, which outlines the issues in this predominantly black district that led to the 1980s anti-police riots. Get off the bus at the **Brixton Station** bus stop, continue on foot for a short distance and turn left into **Electric Avenue.** This street saw frontline action in the 1981 Brixton riots; and Eddy Grant's British reggae classic *Electric Avenue,* released a year later, spells out why the locals felt it was necessary to take to the streets.

● Cross Brixton Road and catch the northbound **59** from the identically named **Brixton Station** stop on the other side. This heads back up through Kennington and Lambeth before crossing **Waterloo Bridge** – scene of possibly the greatest London song of all time. It is over here that lovers Terry and Julie, watched by Ray Davies' slightly sinister narrator, walk in The Kinks' 1967 *Waterloo Sunset*, a beautiful mediation on love, loneliness and the River Thames that has become the city's unofficial national anthem. Bizarrely – considering the band hailed from the north London suburb of Muswell Hill – the song was originally called 'Liverpool Sunset' and was written about the River Mersey. Davies changed the lyrics at the last minute when he recalled watching the sun set over Waterloo Bridge as a child recuperating from illness in St Thomas' Hospital.

● Get off the bus at **Lancaster Place** and catch the northbound **176** from the same stop. This bus immediately turns left onto **the Strand** – subject of the 1908 music-hall song *Let's All Go Down The Strand*, much lampooned for its refrain of 'have a banana' – before turning up St Martin's Lane and Charing Cross Road. The former home of **Central St Martin's College of Art & Design** is located at 102 Charing Cross Road, on the left next to the Montagu Pyke pub. It was a meeting here in 1988 between fine art and film student Jarvis Cocker and a well-to-do Greek girl intrigued by his

Waterloo sunset

Sheffield accent that inspired one of the finest pop-music couplets ever – 'She came from Greece, she had a thirst for knowledge/She studied sculpture at St Martin's College' from Pulp's 1995 song *Common People*.

● Get off the bus at the **Denmark Street** stop, walk back down Charing Cross Road and turn right into Old Compton Street. You are now in **Soho** – one of the most musically celebrated areas in London. This tight network of narrow streets, home to hundreds of bars, clubs and restaurants, has inspired everything from The Pogues' *A Rainy Night in Soho* and Bert Jansch and John Renbourn's *Soho* to Warren Zevon's *Werewolves of London*. Continue walking along Old Compton Street then turn right into Frith Street. You will immediately pass **Bar Italia** – the post-club coffee bar 'where all the ragged people' go in the 1995 Pulp song of the same name – before walking up to **Soho Square**. This small green space is the subject of Kirsty MacColl's song of rejection *Soho Square*. And, following the singer's untimely death in 2000, a bench engraved with the lyrics from this song – 'One day I'll be waiting there/No empty bench in Soho Square' – was installed in the park as a memorial.

● Walk around Soho Square and up Soho Street, then cross Oxford Street and turn right. Catch the northbound **10, 73** or **390** from the **Tottenham Court Road Station** stop, immediately passing the tube station namechecked in Underworld's 1995 dance anthem *Born Slippy*. As the bus heads up Tottenham Court Road, look out for **Goodge Street tube** on the left. It is here, on the Northern Line's 'firefly platform', that Donovan set his 1966 countercultural classic *Sunny Goodge Street* – later covered by Marianne Faithfull. Get off the bus at the **Euston Station** stop. The railway terminus in front of you, which serves Britain's northwest, features in The Smiths' song *London*, the fear-tinged tale of a boy leaving his girlfriend and family behind in Manchester for a new life in the capital.

● Bear right as you exit the small bus station, cross Euston Road and take a short ride on the westbound **30** from the **Euston Station** stop on the other side. Get off the bus at the **York Street** stop – which, despite its name, is situated on **Baker Street**. As well as being the fictional home to Sherlock Holmes, this road's other major claim to fame is the 1978 Gerry Rafferty hit *Baker Street* – which sold more than four million copies

Bar Italia, Frith
Street, Soho

across the world. The song's world-weary tone was the result of the acrimonious break-up of Rafferty's former band Stealer's Wheel, when the singer was forced to travel regularly from his Glasgow home to lawyers' meetings in London. His sanctuary at this time was a friend's flat on Baker Street where he could escape the bitter legal dispute with his record label and ex-bandmates, and concentrate on simply playing music.

● Cross the road and walk along Bickenhall Street to Gloucester Place. Go over to the other side and turn left, then catch the northbound **274** from the **Marylebone Road** bus stop. This bus curls around the outside edge of Regent's Park before passing **Primrose Hill** on the left. It was on this mound that Paul McCartney was walking in 1967 when a spectral man appeared out of the fog and then mysteriously melted away. McCartney was understandably disturbed by this experience; and the Beatle went home to write *The Fool On The Hill*, which appeared on the band's *Magical Mystery Tour* EP. The parkland has also inspired many other tunes – most notably *Primrose Hill* by John and Beverley Martyn (sampled by Fatboy Slim for his track *NW3*) and the identically named song by Loudon Wainwright III, about being homeless amid this picturesque greenery. Billy Bragg's *Upfield* channels the spirit of 18th-century poet William Blake, who believed he saw angels on this hillside.

● Continue on the 274 into Camden and get off at the **Camden Town/Camden Road** stop. Cross over the road, bear right and catch the southbound **C2** from the **Camden Street** stop. This bus heads back into central London around the opposite side of Regent's Park, and goes along Regent Street before turning right into the upmarket district of **Mayfair** – 'even trees are wealthy here,' noted Nick Drake – and around **Berkeley Square.** It is this leafy green space that provides the backdrop to the two lovers in the 1939 classic *A Nightingale Sang in Berkeley Square*. Recorded by everyone from Frank Sinatra and Nat King Cole to Rod Stewart and Harry Connick Jr, the song has become one of popular music's great standards. Though it's as British as teacups and Victoria sponge, it was actually co-written by an Englishman and an American in the Var region of France.

● Continue on the C2 to the **Green Park Station** stop, which is situated in front of the tube station.

To download this journey to your Smartphone, scan the QR code (right)

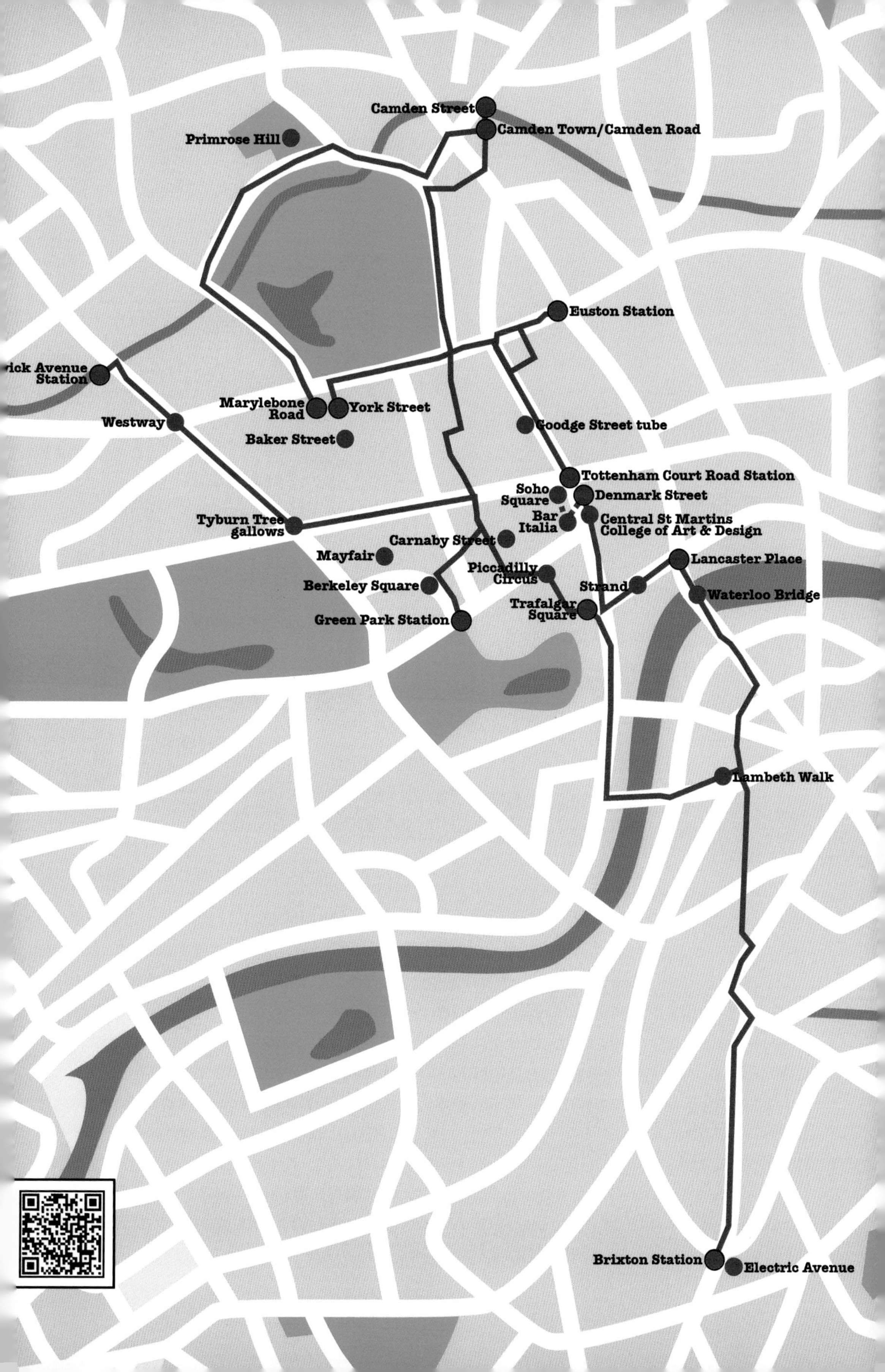
Camden Street
Camden Town/Camden Road
Primrose Hill
Euston Station
rick Avenue Station
Marylebone Road
York Street
Westway
Goodge Street tube
Baker Street
Tottenham Court Road Station
Soho Square
Denmark Street
Bar Italia
Central St Martins College of Art & Design
Tyburn Tree gallows
Carnaby Street
Mayfair
Lancaster Place
Piccadilly Circus
Berkeley Square
Strand
Waterloo Bridge
Trafalgar Square
Green Park Station
Lambeth Walk
Brixton Station
Electric Avenue

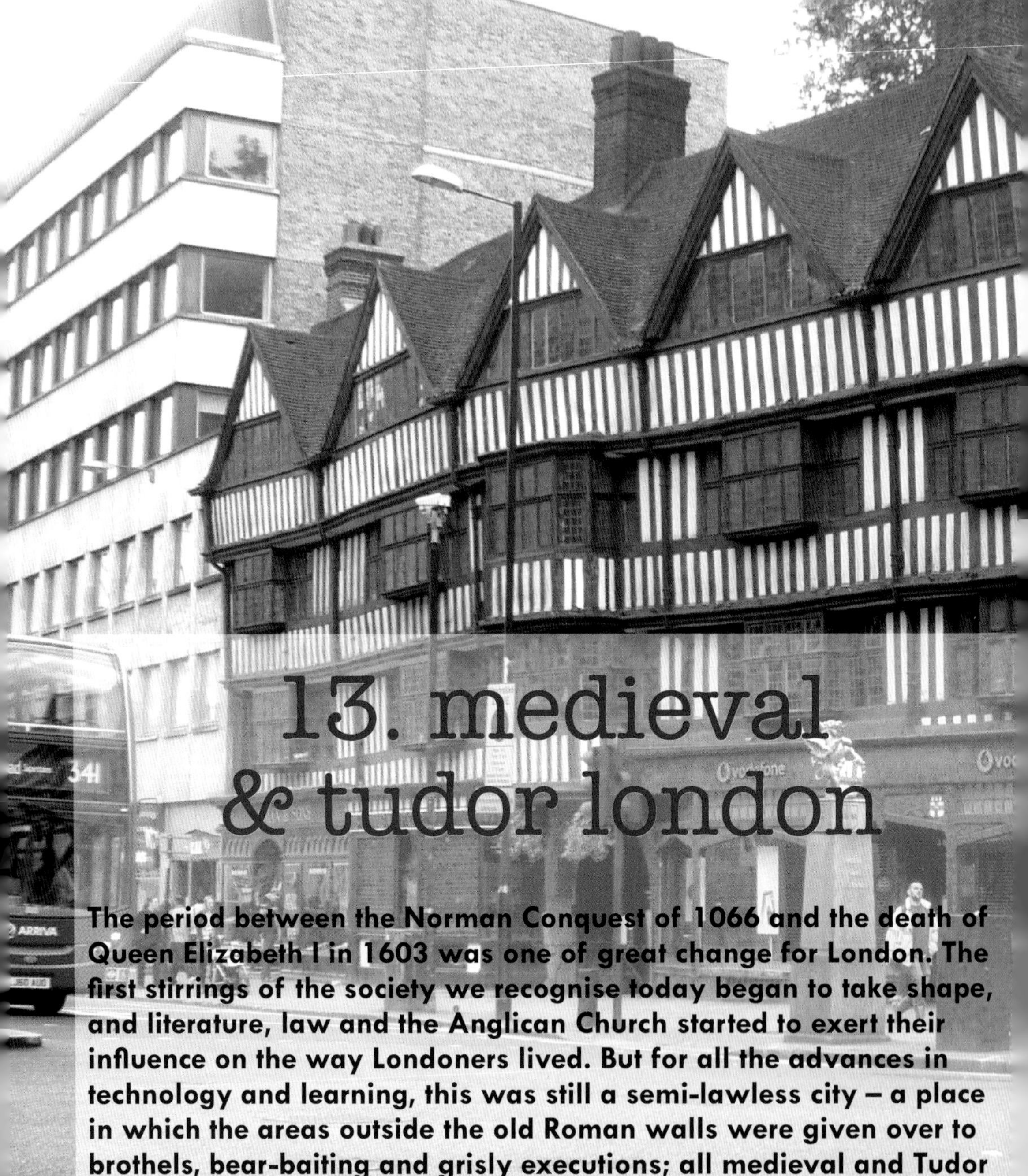

13. medieval & tudor london

The period between the Norman Conquest of 1066 and the death of Queen Elizabeth I in 1603 was one of great change for London. The first stirrings of the society we recognise today began to take shape, and literature, law and the Anglican Church started to exert their influence on the way Londoners lived. But for all the advances in technology and learning, this was still a semi-lawless city – a place in which the areas outside the old Roman walls were given over to brothels, bear-baiting and grisly executions; all medieval and Tudor Londoners' idea of a good day out. Though the Great Fire of 1666 destroyed much of the capital those people would have known, the city still reveals tantalising glimpses of their world.

Tudor buildings at Staple Inn, High Holborn

Start point: Farringdon tube
End point: Chancery Lane tube
Duration: 4 hours

● Come out of **Farringdon tube** and turn left down Cowcross Street. Walk straight through the market to emerge in Smithfield – home to the stunning Tudor gatehouse of St Bartholomew the Great. In medieval times, this open space lay just beyond the city walls, which meant it was not subject to the same laws as the boroughs within. Not only was Smithfield the venue for the annual Bartholomew Fair – a cloth market that grew to become a riotous pleasure zone of sideshows, acrobats, freaks and music – between 1133 and 1855, but it also was a notorious execution site. Hundreds were burnt at the stake here.

● Death and Smithfield seemed to go hand in hand throughout the medieval and Tudor era. When the Black Death carried off around a third of London's population in 1348-49, many of the dead were buried in a mass grave here. And it was to this space that Wat Tyler and his army of 20,000 peasants marched in 1381 to negotiate with King Richard II over unpopular taxes. The Peasants' Revolt was brought to an abrupt end, though, when Tyler was murdered in front of the crowd by the Lord Mayor of London.

● Head to the far right-hand corner of Smithfield and walk down Giltspur Street. Like Smithfield, **Cock Lane** – on the right – wasn't subject to City laws. Known as Cokkes Lane in medieval times, it was where London's legalised brothels were to be found. It had a sordid reputation. Any woman convicted of prostitution within the city walls was marched through Cheapside and Newgate in a striped cap to guarded lodgings on this street.

● Retrace your steps to Smithfield and turn right into the alley between the Tudor gatehouse and St Bartholomew's Hospital. Carry on along Little Britain, then turn left at Montague Street and catch the eastbound **100** from the **Little Britain** stop. This bus then heads along **Houndsditch** – so named because this former moat around the city wall was where Londoners would dump their dead animals.

● Get off the bus at the **Tower Hill/Tower Gateway** stop, walk back up Mansell Street and turn left onto Shorter Street. This takes you to the **Tower of London,** which is where England's first Norman king William the Conqueror built a fortress to keep an eye on his new subjects. William's White Tower was built in 1078, and the complex was further extended in the 12th and 13th centuries. It served as both a

Shrine to the 'Winchester geese' at Crossbones Graveyard, Borough

royal residence and – most infamously – a prison. Henry VIII's wives Anne Boleyn and Catherine Howard were both beheaded within its grounds, while many other important figures – including Thomases More and Cromwell – were executed at **Tower Hill**, just outside its walls.

● Walk back to the junction of Tower Hill and Minories, and turn left. Catch the westbound **RV1** from the **Tower Gateway** stop and take it all the way to the **Hop Exchange** stop by Borough Market. When you get off the bus, walk back up Southwark Street and turn right down Borough High Street. At the junction, cross the road and turn left. **Talbot Yard,** on the right, was where The Tabard Inn – the pub in which Chaucer's pilgrims gather in *The Canterbury Tales* – was situated between 1307 and 1873.

● Return to the Hop Exchange stop and continue walking down Southwark Street, then turn left down Redcross Way. The gates on the left – the bars of which are hung with ribbons, tinsel, plastic flowers and scraps of poetry – are a rudimentary shrine that marks the entrance to what was **Crossbones Graveyard** – a 16th-century unconsecrated cemetery for 'single women', a Tudor euphemism for prostitutes. This is where many of the Winchester Geese – women who worked in brothels licensed by the Bishop of Winchester – were buried outside of church ceremony. The bishop oversaw a semi-lawless state known as The Liberty of the Clink, which sat outside both the City of London and the County of Surrey, and the district was known in medieval and Tudor times as a place of prostitution, theatre and bear-baiting – all forbidden on the other side of the river.

● Return once more to the **Hop Exchange** stop and catch the westbound **RV1**. This runs parallel to Bankside, where a recreation of Shakespeare's Globe Theatre stands close to where bear- and bull-baiting arenas existed in the Tudor era. A street called Bear Gardens, just west of Southwark Bridge, is a reminder of how the area was once synonymous with this bloody form of entertainment.

● Get off the bus at the **Waterloo Station/York Road** stop and catch the westbound **77** from the identically named stop a little further down the road. Get off the bus at **Lambeth Palace**. Still the official residence of the Archbishop of Canterbury, this palace has been the Primate's home since the 1200s and features some fine medieval and Tudor architecture. Its brick gatehouse, for example, dates from 1495. It was from here that Archbishop Thomas

St Bartholomew the Great, Smithfield

Cranmer and Henry VIII's right-hand man Thomas Cromwell orchestrated the Reformation in the early 16th century.

● Continue down Lambeth Palace Road and turn left at the roundabout into Lambeth Road. Catch the northbound **3** from the **Lambeth Palace** stop, and take it across the bridge to the **Parliament Square** stop on Whitehall. As you approach Parliament Square, look to the left for the 14th-century **Jewel Tower. Westminster Abbey,** just behind, is one of the largest and most famous Gothic buildings in the world. The present building was constructed from 1245. All British monarchs, from Harold and William I in 1066 to Queen Elizabeth II in 1953 have been crowned here. And many medieval and Tudor royals – including Anne of Cleves and Elizabeth I – are buried inside.

● Catch the eastbound **11** from the same bus stop. As the bus goes along **Fleet Street,** look to the right for the **Inner Temple Gateway,** which is believed to have been here since the 12th century – though the current gate is a 17th century reproduction. **Prince Henry's Room,** the half-timbered Tudor house that stands over the gate, was one of the few secular buildings to be spared by the Great Fire of London in 1666.

● Get off the bus at **Bank Station/ Threadneedle Street,** walk back down Threadneedle Street, turn hard left into Cornhill and catch the westbound **25** from the **Bank Station/Cornhill** stop. This heads along Cheapside – the City's market place in the medieval times. On the left immediately after Old Jewry (the medieval Jewish ghetto) was where the wonderfully named Gropecunt Alley was located. It was flanked by Puppekirty ('poke skirt') Lane and Bordhawelane (bordello lane), which suggests this was once a miniature red-light district.

● Once you've passed the former Newgate Prison on the corner of Old Bailey, get off the bus at the **Holborn Circus/Fetter Lane** stop. Cross to the othe side of High Holborn and turn right, then turn left into Hatton Garden. Finish your journey with a drink in Ye Olde Mitre – reached by turning down an alleyway on the right. Established in the 1500s, the pub is a suitably historical place in which t toast your medieval and Tudor forebear Though its interiors are more Victorian tha Elizabethan, the Virgin Queen is said to have once danced around the cherry tre that now supports the front of the buildin

To download this journey to your Smartphone, scan the QR code (right)

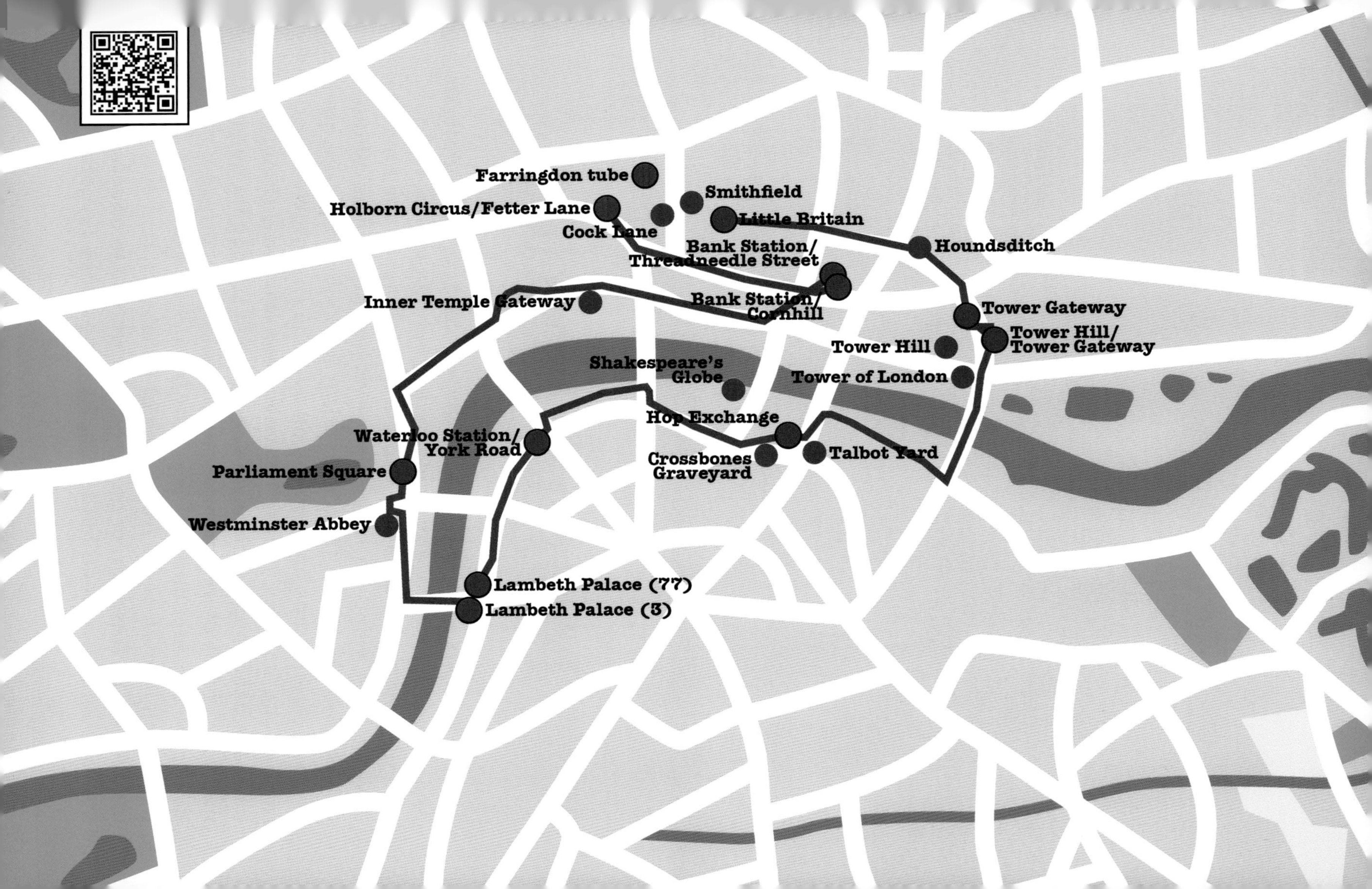
Farringdon tube
Smithfield
Holborn Circus/Fetter Lane
Little Britain
Cock Lane
Houndsditch
Bank Station/
Threadneedle Street
Inner Temple Gateway
Bank Station/
Cornhill
Tower Gateway
Tower Hill/
Tower Gateway
Tower Hill
Shakespeare's
Globe
Tower of London
Hop Exchange
Waterloo Station/
York Road
Crossbones
Graveyard
Talbot Yard
Parliament Square
Westminster Abbey
Lambeth Palace (77)
Lambeth Palace (3)

14. gay london

London today is a largely tolerant city – accepting of all lifestyles and cultures – and the gay scene here is out and proud. The gay centres around Vauxhall and Old Compton Street in Soho may be the obvious focal points for homosexual visitors (as well as outraged *Daily Mail* readers keen for a voyeuristic peek), but there are hundreds of bars, clubs, shops and saunas all over the city targeted specifically at gays and lesbians. It hasn't always been this way. Though there has been a thriving homosexual subculture in London for hundreds – if not thousands – of years, it has traditionally been driven underground due to the constant threat of reprisals from church and state, where it developed its own codes and styles of behaviour, and even its own language. The freedom for gay men and women to openly celebrate their sexuality has been hard-won. As this journey reveals.

Start point: Bank tube
End point: Leicester Square tube
Duration: 3.5 hours

● Come out of Exit 1 at **Bank tube** and follow the signs to Poultry. Continue up the road before crossing over and catching the westbound **8, 25** or **242** from the **Poultry/Bank Station** stop. All these buses immediately head along **Cheapside**, the City's market district in medieval times. It was here that cross-dressing male prostitute John Rykener was arrested by constables in 1395. The record of Rykener's interrogation by the mayor and aldermen of London is the only existing medieval legal document concerning same-sex intercourse, so it's just as well its contents are fairly fruity. As well as being found 'committing that detestable, unmentionable and ignominious vice' (ie, oral sex with another man) in a public place, Rykener also admitted to having sex with a long list of scholars and priests in return for money; he preferred clergymen, though, as they tended to pay better.

● Though there are no records of what happened to Rykener after his interrogation, it is likely he received some punishment for lewd behaviour. Homosexual men were strongly disapproved of by a strongly religious society and he may well have been placed in one of the city's pillories or stocks. The Buggery Act of 1533 introduced the death penalty for anyone found guilty of having anal sex, though this sentence was rarely passed by judges. But, as you pass the site of **Newgate Prison** – to the left, on the corner of Newgate Street and Old Bailey – it's worth remembering that several cases did end with the defendant's death. The last executions for buggery took place at the prison as late as 1835, when John Smith and John Pratt were hanged after being convicted of having sex in a house in Southwark. The act remained in force for another 25 years, though no one else proved to be quite so unlucky.

● The bus continues across Holborn Viaduct. Just after it crosses Farringdon Road – the main street beneath – look out for **Shoe Lane**, which runs parallel to it. It was on this street that 'Mother' Margaret Clap operated her Molly House in the early 18th century. Blurring the line between tavern and brothel, Mother Clap's Molly House was a place in which 'mollies' (gay men in the slang of the time) of all social classes could meet, drink and indulge in sexual activity away from the eyes of the law. The house was raided, though, in 1726 and more than 40 men were arrested along with their hostess. Clap, who was pilloried at Smithfield for her troubles, became the subject of Mark Ravenhill's play *Mother Clap's Molly House*, which debuted at the National Theatre in 2001.

● Just after the bus passes Holborn tube, look to the left for a glimpse of **The Princess Louise** pub. This Victorian tavern was one of the bars that gay serial killer Dennis Nilsen used to pick up his victims in the late 1970s and early 1980s. Specifically targeting students, the homeless or itinerant workers, he would meet men in the pub then invite them back to his homes in Cricklewood and Muswell Hill. Here he would ply them with alcohol, kill them and store the body under the floorboards. He was only caught when he called out a company to unblock his drain, and the repair man found it stuffed with human flesh.

● Get off the bus at the **High Holborn** stop and walk back towards Holborn tube. Turn right down Kingsway and catch the northbound **59, 68, 91, 168** or **188** from the **Holborn Station** stop. Get off the bus at the **Russell Square Station** stop, walk back and turn left into Coram Street. Turn left at the end of the road and walk up Marchmount Street to **Gay's The Word** – the capital's best-known gay and lesbian bookshop, which has been selling everything from cutting-edge queer theory to gay erotic fiction here since 1979.

● Continue up Marchmount Street then turn left onto Tavistock Place. After a minute or so, turn right into Tavistock Square and catch the southbound **91** from the **Tavistock Square** stop. This bus heads down Kingsway and around Aldwych onto the Strand. Get off at the **Bedford Street** stop and walk back along **the Strand,** which was something of a cruising ground in the 18th century. Pause for a moment at **Savoy Court** on the right. As the brown plaques attached to the pillars inside the alleyway state, this was the location of the Fountain Tavern – one of the most notorious gay pubs of the Georgian era.

● Continue back along the Strand and catch the southbound **59** from the **Aldwych/Somerset House** stop, which is in front of King's College. This bus takes you over Waterloo Bridge and into the south London district of Kennington. Get off at the **Kennington Church** stop, then walk back up the road, turn right onto Camberwell New Road and catch the northbound **36** from the **Kennington**

Gay's The Word bookshop,
Marchmount Street

Park stop. After passing The Oval cricket ground, the bus starts making its way through Vauxhall gay village. While village is too grandiose a term – even 'hamlet' doesn't really do it justice – there are a few gay bars, clubs and shops situated beneath the railway arches. The area's crowning glory, though, is the **Royal Vauxhall Tavern**, which is on the right-hand side. This nightclub-cum-cabaret venue has been a gay hangout since the 1940s and was a favourite of Freddie Mercury during the 1970s. Its legendary Saturday-night Duckie event has been running for 14 years now.

● Once you've recrossed the River Thames, get off the bus at the **Grosvenor Gardens** stop, continue along the road and then turn left into **Ebury Street**. At the bottom of the road, on the right, you'll see the house in which Mozart wrote his first symphony. Of far more interest to lesbian tourists, however, is **number 182** next door. This is where author, poet and gardener Vita Sackville-West had her famous affair with Virginia Woolf in the late 1920s, as well as several other liaisons with women on the fringes of the Bloomsbury Set.

● At the bottom of Ebury Street, turn right along Pimlico Road and then right again up Lower Sloane Street. When you reach Sloane Square, turn right and catch the northbound **C1** from the **Sloane Square Station** stop. When the bus heads up Sloane Street, look to the left for the **Cadogan Hotel**, which is on the corner of Pavilion Street. It was here, in 1895, that Oscar Wilde was arrested for 'committing acts of gross indecency with other male persons' following the collapse of the libel trial he had brought against the Marquis of Queensberry. He was sentenced to two years hard labour in Reading Gaol for the crime.

● Get off the bus at the **Knightsbridge Station/Harrods** stop, cross the road and turn right. Catch the northbound **14** from the **Knightsbridge Station** stop. **Piccadilly**, which the bus enters after passing Hyde Park Corner, was well-known as a street frequented by male prostitutes in the 19th century. Indeed, Morrissey used this subject matter for his 1990 song *Piccadilly Palare*. The 'palare' or – as it's more usually known – 'polari' he refers to is the secret language used in London's gay subculture from the 1600s until the late 1960s. This slang, which incorporates elements of Italian, Cockney, Yiddish and Romany, was essential for communication at a time when homosexuality was punishable by

Old Compton Street, Soho

death. Certain polari words – most notably 'naff' and 'camp' – have now become incorporated into standard English.

● Just after the bus passes Green Park and The Ritz hotel, look left for **Albemarle Street**. This is where Oscar Wilde's Albemarle Club was located (at number 13), and where the Marquis of Queensberry (father of Wilde's supposed lover Alfred Douglas) left a card stating 'For Oscar Wilde, posing somdomite [sic]' – the slander which began the events that led to Wilde's downfall.

● As the bus heads up Shaftesbury Avenue, look to the right for a glimpse of **Haymarket** at the other end of Great Windmill Street. As at other sites across London, most notably at Charing Cross and on Floral Street in Covent Garden, Haymarket was the location of a pillory. And it was here, in 1810, that six members of the Vere Street Coterie – a group of men arrested for sodomy in a Holborn molly house – were placed in a stocks-like contraption in front of a particularly vicious crowd, which hurled dead cats, rotten fish and vegetables at them over several hours. They were the lucky ones. Two more members of the coterie were hanged at Newgate Prison six months later.

● Get off the bus at the **Denmark Street** stop, walk back down Charing Cross Road and turn right into **Old Compton Street**. You are now walking along the road that marks the centre of modern gay London. Almost every business along this street is aimed exclusively at a homosexual clientele, and those that aren't are gay-friendly to the point of getting a bit over-familiar. Rainbow pride flags hang in most windows, men and women openly hold hands and kiss in the street, and high-end coffee bars stand next to low-rent sex shops. There is even a dedicated Gay Tourist Office on the corner of Frith Street, which provides information for gay visitors to the capital. Finish your journey at the iconic **Admiral Duncan** pub, about halfway along the street on the right. This was the pub in which a nailbomb was detonated by a neo-Nazi terrorist in 1999, killing three customers. The pub reopened nine weeks later following a ceremony attended by hundreds, and now incorporates a chandelier that features three candles to commemorate the dead and 86 twinkling bulbs to remember the injured. It's the latest significant monument in the city's long and turbulent gay history.

To download this journey to your Smartphone, scan the QR code (right)

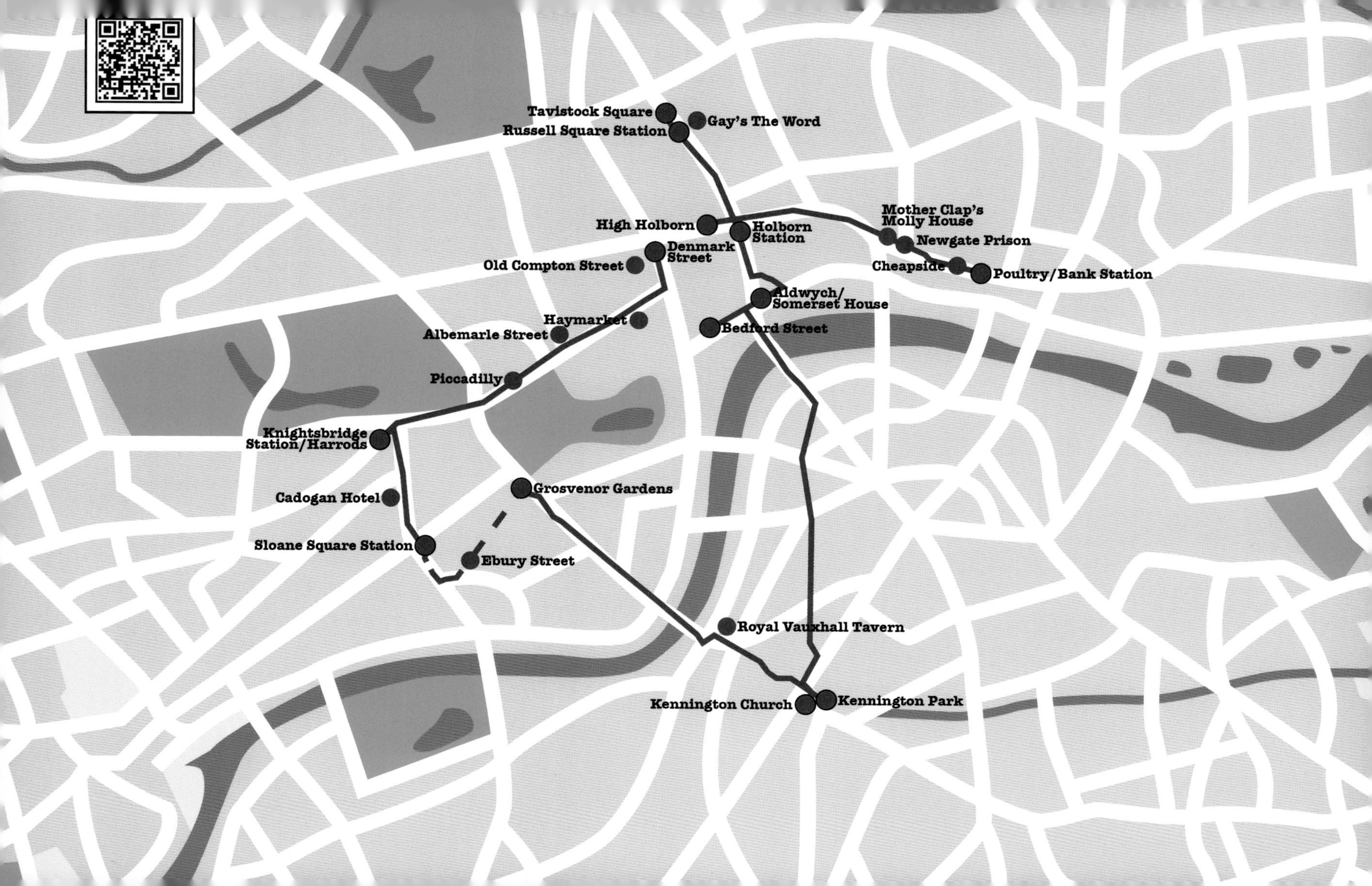
Tavistock Square
Gay's The Word
Russell Square Station
High Holborn
Holborn Station
Mother Clap's Molly House
Newgate Prison
Cheapside
Poultry/Bank Station
Denmark Street
Old Compton Street
Aldwych/ Somerset House
Haymarket
Bedford Street
Albemarle Street
Piccadilly
Knightsbridge Station/Harrods
Grosvenor Gardens
Cadogan Hotel
Sloane Square Station
Ebury Street
Royal Vauxhall Tavern
Kennington Church
Kennington Park

15. a passage to india

Centuries of trade plus nearly 90 years as the jewel in the crown of the British Empire created strong links between India and the UK. And when independence was granted in 1947 – and the country was carved up along religious lines into present-day India, Pakistan and Bangladesh – many former subjects of the Crown headed to the motherland in search of a better life. in London, as in other British industrial cities, clearly defined Asian districts began to form. This journey takes you around some of the capital's most vibrant Indian, Pakistani and Bangladeshi areas; places that retain a strong cultural identity originally forged thousands of miles away.

Shree Sanatan
Mandir, Wembley

Start point: Southall overground
End point: Liverpool Street tube
Duration: 4.5 hours

● When you get off the train at **Southall overground**, the first thing you'll notice is the bilingual signs – in English and Gurmuki, the written form of Punjabi – which are the first clue this district is as every bit as Indian as it is British. When you come out of the station, cross the road and turn right. Catch the northbound **105, 120, 195, E5** or **H32** – passing the building that used to house the **Glassy Junction** pub on the right. Until it closed in early 2012, this Punjabi inn, which even accepted payment in rupees, was one of Southall's most famous landmarks – having made several appearances in Bollywood movies.

● The first Indians arrived in Southall in 1950 to take up jobs in a factory owned by a former British Indian Army officer. The proximity of Heathrow Airport and the jobs created by its expansion in the 1950s led to further waves of immigration, and the area became predominantly South Asian by the 1970s. The population is mainly Sikh and Hindu, though the district is also home to a significant number of Pakistani Muslims; and this cultural mix is evident as soon as you step onto the bus. As well as your fellow passengers – who are most likely to be speaking in Punjabi or Urdu – you will be surrounded by glimpses of India wherever you turn. Look out for the ornate **Himalaya Palace** cinema on the left, which is a wonderfully faded Asian-inspired architectural gem amid the scruffy shops and cafés of South Road. There can be few places in London more appropriate a setting for the Bollywood films that are screened regularly here.

● Get off the bus at the **Southall Broadway** stop and continue walking up to the junction. Southall Broadway, which stretches to the left and right of here, is lined with Indian grocers, restaurants and other businesses, and from around 10am you'll see grills and miniature ovens being set up on the pavement to send out delicious aromas into the air. The UK's high-street chains also have a strong presence here, yet the likes of Gregg's and Costa make an incongruous sight when wreathed in spice-infused steam. If you're here on a Wednesday, Friday or Saturday, turn right and walk along to **Southall Market** which is like stepping into the streets of Mumbai. Sizzling outdoor grills and stalls piled high with fresh chillies are packed

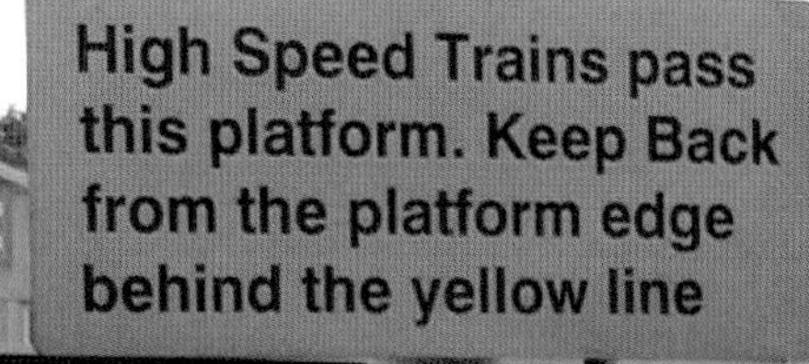
High Speed Trains pass
this platform. Keep Back
from the platform edge
behind the yellow line

in next to glittering boards of gold jewellery and racks of primary-coloured saris. What with all the sight, sounds and smells, it's very easy to forget you're in west London.

● Catch the eastbound **195**, **207** or **427** from the **Southall Police Station** bus stop, which is opposite the entrance to the market. Get off at **Ealing Hospital** and, from the same stop, take the northbound **83** all the way up to **Clayton Avenue**. Get off the bus and walk back down Ealing Road to the **Shree Sanatan Mandir**, which is situated on the right. This beautiful Hindu limestone temple, which cost £16 million and was built using only traditional techniques, took 14 years to construct and opened its doors as recently as 2010. Many of intricate designs that cover its walls and towers were hand-carved in the Indian province of Gujarat and flown to the UK; and it contains 41 marble deities – including one of Mother Theresa – which were specially sculpted in India for the building.

● Upon leaving the temple complex, turn left at the exit and walk up Ealing Road. The parade of shops here provides Wembley's mainly Gujarati Hindu community with all the South Asian clothing, foodstuffs and other reminders of their ancestral home they could possibly require. It's reassuringly noisy and colourful. Cross the road so you're on the opposite side to the Shree Sanatan Mandir and walk up to the **Eagle Road** bus stop. Catch the eastbound **224** from here to the **Swaminarayan Temple** stop on Brentfield Road in Neasden.

● Get off the bus right next to the stunning **Shri Swaminarayan Mandir** (better known as Neasden Temple), which was built in the 1990s as a focal point for northwest London's Hindu communities. Constructed from nearly 5,000 tonnes of Bulgarian limestone and Italian marble, it is the largest Hindu temple outside India. To visit its sumptuous interior, which includes seven separate shrines beneath each of its pinnacles, as well as an adjoining cultural centre and exhibition centre, you need to enquire at the reception desk inside the main entrance. But – be warned – though the temple claims to be open 365 days a year, you may arrive (as this writer did) to find all gates securely closed and no sign of anyone to admit you. Whether you get in or not, though, the temple is still an awe-inspiring sight.

● Cross the road and catch the southbound **206** or **224** from the

aling Road, Wembley

Swaminarayan Temple stop down to **Knatchbull Road**. Walk back up to the junction, cross the main road and turn right to catch the eastbound **18** from the identically named **Knatchbull Road** stop on the A404. This bus goes through Harlesden, Kensal Green and Maida Vale – home to small Portuguese and Middle Eastern communities – before heading alongside the Westway and up Marylebone Road. Get off at the **Euston Station** terminus.

● Catch the eastbound **205** from the bus station in the railway station forecourt – it goes from stop D, which is situated directly in front of a branch of Nando's. This bus takes you through Islington and down City Road, before skirting the old City of London and heading up towards Whitechapel – a traditionally Jewish district that is now home to a predominantly Bangladeshi population. Indeed, London's East End, of which Whitechapel marks the western frontier, has been the focus of successive waves of immigration from Bangladesh and Pakistan, and there are large, well-established Muslim communities everywhere from East Ham to Bethnal Green.

● Get off the bus at the **Osborn Street** stop, then walk back down Whitechapel Road and turn right into Osborn Street. This leads up to **Brick Lane**, the centre of London's Banglatown, around which families from the country's Greater Sylhet region began to settle from the 1970s onwards. A fabulous mix of Bangladeshi cafés, restaurants and shops, and boutiques and galleries that have sprung up around the fashionable east London art scene (with a handful of remnants from its days as a Jewish enclave), Brick Lane is one of the most fascinating streets in the capital. But despite all the young hipsters in directional outfits wandering between its trendy bars and exhibition spaces, this is still a traditional South Asian Islamic community. At its heart is the Jamme Masjid mosque, and signs – even the ones denoting the names of streets – are in Bengali as well as English

● Once you've explored Brick Lane, turn into Fournier Street – which runs alongside the mosque – and walk to Commercial Street. Bear left across the road and continue up Brushfield Street, which flanks Old Spitalfields Market, to emerge on Bishopsgate. Cross the road and turn left to get to **Liverpool Street tube**.

To download this journey to your Smartphone, scan the QR code (right)

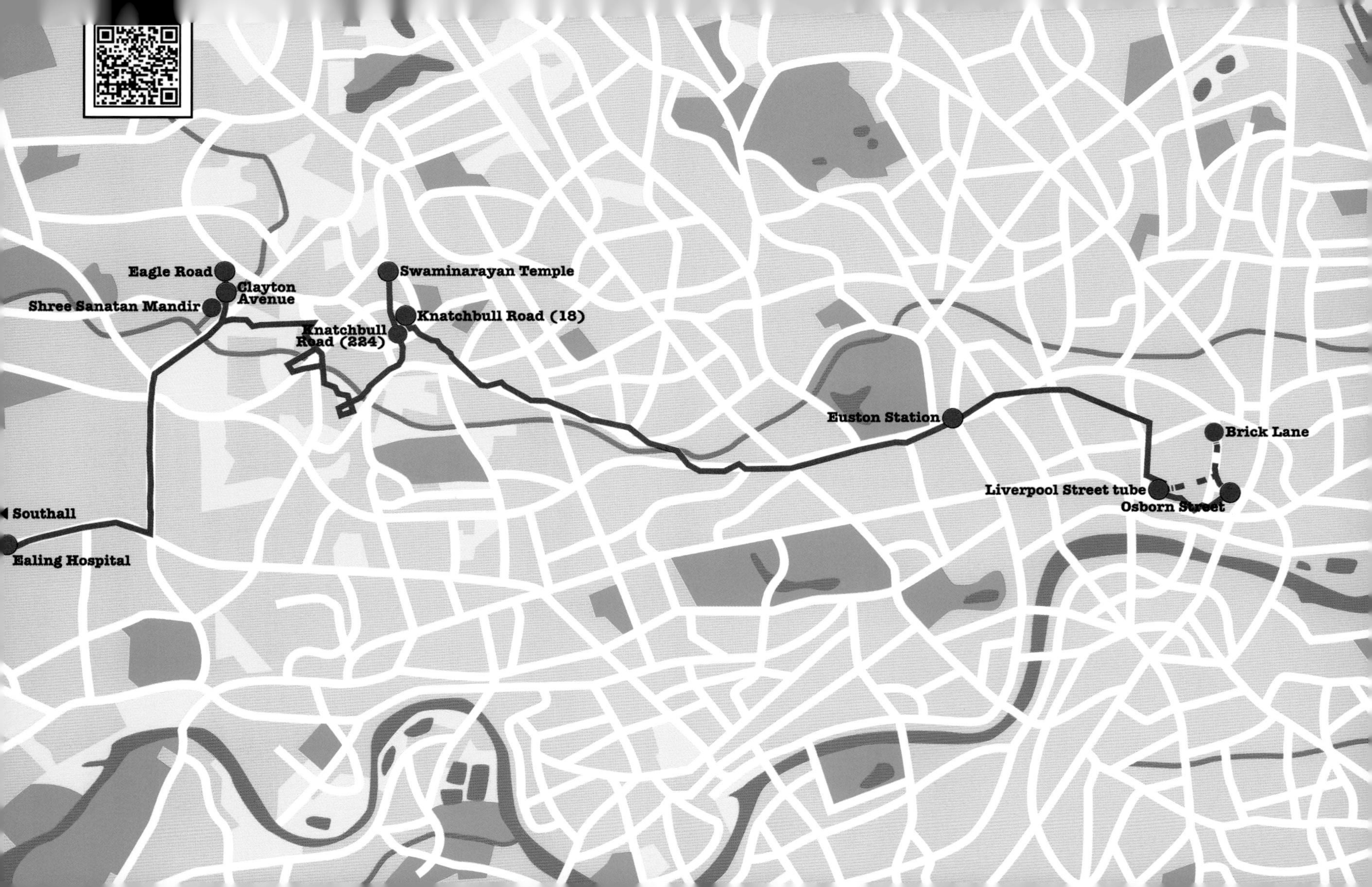

Ealing Hospital
Southall
Shree Sanatan Mandir
Eagle Road
Clayton Avenue
Knatchbull Road (224)
Swaminarayan Temple
Knatchbull Road (18)
Euston Station
Liverpool Street tube
Osborn Street
Brick Lane

16. london on film

From rom-coms to horror, fantasy to kitchen-sink drama, London has starred in many movies over the years. With an ambience that changes from one postcode to another – and often several times in between – the city is one of the greatest character actors in the business. It has played the bustling boho backdrop to Hugh Grant and Julia Roberts' improbable romance in *Notting Hill* and made a convincing wartorn Saigon in *Full Metal Jacket*. It has shown its seamier side in *The Long Good Friday* and *Lock, Stock and Two Smoking Barrels*, yet put in convincing performances as a magical, child-friendly playground in *Mary Poppins* and the *Harry Potter* series. In honour of its Oscar-worthy career, this journey takes you to where some of the most iconic movies to be shot in the capital were made. The list of London film locations is endless, so think of this trip as a director's cut...

Start point: Putney Bridge tube
End point: Camden Town tube
Duration: 5 hours

● Come out of **Putney Bridge tube** and bear right around Station Approach onto Gonville Street. This emerges onto the north side of Putney Bridge opposite **All Saint's Church**, which appeared in 1976 horror film *The Omen*. It was from this church spire that a lightning rod, dislodged by a storm, falls down to impale Patrick Troughton's priest Father Brennan through the neck.

● Cross the road and turn left, then catch the northbound **14** or **22** from the **Putney Bridge Station/Gonville Street** stop. Get off the bus at the **Piccadilly Circus** stop and continue along Piccadilly to London's most famous roundabout. It was here that director John Landis filmed the final climactic scenes of his 1981 comedy-horror classic *An American Werewolf in London*. The chaotic ending, in which David Naughton's lycanthrope runs amok in Piccadilly Circus, was shot in two three-hour bursts. Landis – who had persuaded local police to allow filming by putting on a Met-only screening of his previous film *The Blues Brothers* at a nearby cinema – managed to achieve one of the iconic London movie moments despite only being allowed to stop traffic three times for a maximum of two minutes.

● From Piccadilly Circus, turn left into Regent Street. Cross the road and catch the eastbound **15** from the **Piccadilly Circus** stop. Once the bus has passed through Trafalgar Square and onto the Strand, look to the right for **The Savoy Hotel** – where Bob Hoskins has his final meeting with the Mafia before being abducted by Pierce Brosnan's IRA hitman in *The Long Good Friday*. **Australia House**, on the right at the eastern end of Aldwych, stood in for the goblin-run Gringott's Bank in *Harry Potter And The Philosopher's Stone*, while **The Royal Courts of Justice** – on the left as the bus enters Fleet Street – is where barrister Mark Darcy helps hapless TV reporter Bridget Jones get a scoop in 2001's *Bridget Jones's Diary*.

● Get off the bus at the **Monument Station** stop, walk back along Cheapside and turn right up Gracechurch Street. **Leadenhall Market**, a short walk up the road on the right, stood in for Diagon Alley – the shopping street for witches and wizards – in all the Harry Potter films. The market also features prominently in *The Imaginarium of Doctor*

Parnassus, the last film that Australian actor Heath Ledger made before his death in 2008.

● Leave the market through its Gracechurch Street exit and turn left. Walk down to the **Fenchurch Street** stop and catch the southbound **35**, which heads over **London Bridge** – the bridge that Hugh Grant crosses as commuters flow the other way in 2002's *About A Boy* – towards Borough Market. Get off at the **Southwark Street** bus stop and walk back up the road, then turn left into Bedale Street. The flat over **The Globe** pub was Renée Zellweger's home in *Bridget Jones's Diary*; a location choice that caused many Londoners to wonder how a character who worked in a low-level publishing job could possibly afford an idyllic property in such a sought-after area. **Borough Market,** which lies behind The Globe, also makes an appearance in *Lock, Stock and Two Smoking Barrels*, *The French Lieutenant's Woman* and *Wilde*.

● Come out of the market, turn right down Southwark Street and catch the westbound **RV1** from the **Hop Exchange** stop. This bus passes along the southern end of **Blackfriars Bridge,** which Sally Hawkins cycles over in the opening sequence of Mike Leigh's 2008 film *Happy Go Lucky*, before passing the concrete buildings of the **Southbank Centre** on its way over Waterloo Bridge. It was on the concourse in front of these that Hugh Grant stutteringly confesses his love for Andie Macdowell – using the lyrics of the Partridge Family – in 1994's *Four Weddings And A Funeral*.

● Get off the bus at the **Covent Garden/ Catherine Street** stop terminus and continue walking around Aldwych and along Fleet Street. Turn right into Inner Temple Gateway (the alley opposite Chancery Lane) and walk down to the circular **Temple Church**. This beautiful 12th-century building, known for its links to the Knights Templar and the lifelike medieval effigies it contains, was visited by Tom Hanks and Audrey Tatou on their whistle-stop tour of Europe's religious buildings in *The Da Vinci Code*.

● Return to Fleet Street, turn right and walk along for a few minutes. Turn right onto New Bridge Street (which leads down to Blackfriars Bridge) and catch the northbound **63** from the **Blackfriars Station/North Entrance** stop. Get off a few minutes later at **Snow Hill,** walk back down Farringdon Street and turn left into West Smithfield. **St**

Temple Church, sta[illegible] of *The Da Vinci Code*

Bartholomew the Great, the church in the far corner of the square at the top, was where Hugh Grant's aborted wedding to Anna Chancellor was held in *Four Weddings And A Funeral*. It was also used as a location in 1991's *Robin Hood: Prince Of Thieves* and 1998's *Shakespeare In Love*.

● Turn around, walk across the front of St Bartholomew's Hospital and down Giltspur Street. At the bottom, cross the road and turn right, then catch the westbound **8** from the **City Thameslink Station** stop. Get off the bus at the **Tottenham Court Road Station** stop right next to **Centre Point**. It is at the foot of this building that Cillian Murphy sets off a car alarm in Danny Boyle's 2002 horror film *28 Days Later*. The tube station here is where a late-night commuter is chased and killed by the werewolf in *American Werewolf in London*. Though the platform shots in the movie are of Tottenham Court Road, the actual chase sequence was filmed in the underground tunnels at nearby Charing Cross.

● Catch the westbound **7** from the same bus stop and take it all the way along **Oxford Street** – another famous London location that Cillian Murphy finds eerily deserted in *28 Days Later* – to Notting Hill. Look right as the bus goes along **Westbourne Park Road** and you will see the house shared by Hugh Grant and Rhys Ifans in 1999's *Notting Hill* at number 280. The house's famous blue door was auctioned off by its owner – the film's writer Richard Curtis – several years ago.

● Get off the bus at the **Ladbroke Grove Station** stop, walk back down Ladbroke Grove and turn left into Westbourne Park Road. Turn right down **Portobello Road**, venue for the Saturday market that was used for several shots in *Notting Hill*, and walk down to number 142. This was the location of Grant's travel bookshop in the film.

● Walk all the way down Portobello Road, turn right down Pembridge Road and catch the eastbound **452** from the **Notting Hill Gate Station** stop. The bus passes the **Albert Memorial** – in which monkey man Christopher Lambert takes refuge after escaping the Natural History Museum in 1984's *Greystoke: The Legend of Tarzan, Lord Of The Apes* – on the left; and, opposite, the Royal Albert Hall, which appears in the climax of both the 1934 and 1956 versions of Alfred Hitchcock's *The Man Who Knew Too Much*. Get off the bus at the **Lister**

Regent's Park from Gloucester Gate, as seen in *Withnail and I*

Hospital stop, just off the Chelsea Embankment, which offers a wonderful view of **Battersea Power Station** on the other side of the river. This iconic Art Deco building has been committed to celluloid several times – most notably as the façade of Victory Mansions in the John Hurt and Richard Burton version of *1984* and as Bosworth battlefield in Ian McKellen's 1995 reworking of Shakespeare's *Richard III*.

● Walk back up Chelsea Bridge Road, turn right onto Pimlico Road and catch the eastbound **211** from the **Chelsea Bridge Road** stop. The bus goes through Parliament Square and past **Big Ben** – which Chevy Chase and his family circle endlessly in 1985's *National Lampoon's European Vacation*, and which is blown up by alien spacecraft in the two 1996 films *Independence Day* and *Mars Attacks!* – before crossing **Westminster Bridge**, the first deserted London location encountered in *28 Days Later*.

● Get off the bus at the **Westminster Bridge/County Hall** stop, then cross the road and catch the northbound **148** from the identically named stop on the other side. Take the bus up to the **Marble Arch** stop, then cross Park Lane, walk up to the top and turn right onto Oxford Street. Cross at the traffic lights, turn right and then left into Portman Street. Catch the northbound **274** from the **Portman Street/Selfridges** stop and take it all the way up to Camden Town. On this final bus ride, you'll pass **London Zoo** on the right, which is where David Naughton wakes up naked in the wolf enclosure in *An American Werewolf in London* and Daniel Radcliffe liberates a boa constrictor in *Harry Potter And The Philosopher's Stone*. The entrance to the zoo also stood in for the main gates of Wimbledon in the eponymous 2004 film – the actual entrance to the tennis tournament was not deemed photogenic enough to be used in the movie. Look to the right just after the zoo, and you will see the path leading from **Gloucester Gate** into Regent's Park upon which Paul McGann and Richard E Grant say their goodbyes at the end of 1987's *Withnail And I*, leaving Grant to recite *Hamlet* to the wolves on the other side of the fence.

● The bus then continues down Parkway and into Camden Town. Get off at the **Camden High Street** stop and carry on walking down the road to the tube.

To download this journey to your Smartphone, scan the QR code (right).

London Zoo
Gloucester Gate
Ladbroke Grove Station
Westbourne Park Road
Portobello Road
Notting Hill Gate Station
Portman Street/ Selfridges
Oxford Street
Tottenham Court Road Station
Marble Arch
Piccadilly Circus
Albert Memorial
Royal Albert Hall
Snow Hill
St Bartholomew the Great
City Thameslink Station
Royal Courts of Justice
Australia House
Covent Garden/ Catherine Street
Blackfriars Station/ North Entrance
Leadenhall Market
Fenchurch Street
Temple Church
Monument Station
Savoy Hotel
Blackfriars Bridge
London Bridge
Southbank Centre
The Globe
Hop Exchange
Southwark Street
Westminster Bridge/ County Hall
Big Ben
Chelsea Bridge Road
Lister Hospital
Battersea Power Station
All Saints Church
Putney Bridge Station/Gonville Street

Phone boxes at Smithfield Meat Market

17. midweek markets

In London, every day is market day. Though the big weekend markets of Portobello, Spitalfields, Borough and Columbia Road (covered elsewhere in this book) are perhaps the best-known – and, for Londoners, provide as much of a focal point for socialising as they do for shopping – the stalls set up in midweek are just as fascinating and browse-worthy. From bustling early morning produce markets from which the city's shopkeepers and restaurateurs stock shelves and fill menus to haphazard collections of pitches that pull in everyone from bargain fashion hunters to workers looking for a cheap lunch, London's markets are as integral to the capital as the tube network. And, as many of them have been selling their wares in the same location since medieval times, they are an anchor of tradition that no amount of urban regeneration can dislodge.

Start point: Farringdon tube
End point: Liverpool Street tube
Duration: 3.5 hours

● If you want to see **Smithfield Market** at its best, you need to get there before 7.00am. Any later and you'll miss out on the scene that has been enacted on this site in central London for around 1,000 years. Trading at this most famous of meat markets begins at 3am, though you'll have to wait for the first tubes to start running at around 5.30am before you can make your way to **Farringdon**. To get to the market, come out of the station and turn left down Cowcross Street. Walk right to the end and you'll emerge opposite the grand Victorian cast-iron structure that has housed what's officially known as London Central Markets since 1868. This was once a livestock market and, from the 10th century onwards, farmers would walk their cows, sheep and poultry hundreds of miles to sell them for the best prices here. Cattle stampeding through the London streets and the inevitable injuries they caused to anyone standing in their way meant that, in the mid-19th century, the market was forced to change to one that specialised in pre-slaughtered meat. Though the danger of trampling has gone, the market is still an exciting place to visit – and not just on days when you're planning a barbecue for the afternoon. For the ultimate Smithfield experience, join the traders at **The Cock Tavern**, which is situated below the market, for a hearty breakfast of sausages, bacon and other prime meat from 6am onwards. Until recently, alcohol was served here from 6.30am – making it as much of a post-club hangout as it was a place for bloodied butchers to rest their cleavers while downing a well-earned pint of Guinness.

● Come out of Smithfield Market on the opposite side to which you entered and walk over to the far corner of the square – to the right of St Bartholomew's Hospital. Turn right and walk down Giltspur Street then turn right onto Holborn Viaduct. Cross over the road and catch the westbound **8** or **25** from the **City Thameslink Station** stop. Once the bus moves onto Oxford Street, get off at the **Wardour Street** stop and continue along the road for a few metres before turning left into **Berwick Street.** The small market at the bottom of here, which specialises mainly in food items, has been operating in the heart of Soho since the 18th century. As snapshots of London life go, it's hard to beat the image you'll find here of traders hawking

Berwick Street Market, Soho

apples, potatoes and fresh fish against a backdrop of neon sex shop signs.

● Walk back up to Oxford Street, turn right and catch either the westbound **8, 10** or **73** from the **Wardour Street** stop, or the westbound **7** or **25** from the identically named stop just a little bit further along the road. Take the bus up to the **Selfridges** stop – opposite the ultimate upmarket and glamorous modern take on the old-fashioned marketplace – and walk back to Bond Street tube station. Turn down Davies Street, the first road on the right after passing the station, and walk down to **Grays antiques market** – housed in a beautiful Victorian terracotta building at number 58. A mecca for dealers and experts, this vast concentration of stalls, which fill two floors and a mews building nearby, holds millions of pounds worth of stock. Everything from toys and trinkets to maps and militaria can be found here, and a lot more besides. You may not find many bargains; but wandering its snaking aisles, gazing into cases and chatting to the passionate and knowledgeable stallholders, makes it well worth the visit.

● Return to Oxford Street, cross over the road and turn right. Turn left after passing the John Lewis department store and catch the eastbound **8** or **25** from the **Holles Street** stop. After travelling the length of Oxford Street and past Holborn tube, get off at the **Brownlow Street** stop on High Holborn, continue walking down the road and turn right into Chancery Lane. **The London Silver Vaults**, which you access by turning left into Southampton Buildings, is one of the city's most secret marketplaces. There's very little to advertise its subterranean presence and visitors have to pass a security guard and go down a flight of stairs before reaching the vaults. The market began life in 1876 as a storage facility for household valuables, but the dealers moved in shortly afterwards. It's exactly as it sounds. The traders here occupy 19th-century strongrooms, throwing open thick doors to reveal glittering collections of silverware from every period and in every style imaginable. The overall feel is of stumbling across a pirate's treasure hoard in a Victorian prison. It's absolutely stunning and rather unearthly.

● Return to High Holborn, cross the road and turn right. Walk for two minutes, then turn left into Leather Lane, the entrance to which is marked by the Sir Christopher Hatton pub. **Leather Lane Market**, which begins just a short stroll beyond here, has

Leadenhall Market

been well-known as a place to pick up cheap goods for more than 300 years. The stalls that line the road from its junction with Hatton Gardens all the way up to Clerkenwell Road sell everything from designer dresses and cut-price underwear to cheap CDs and boxes of past-its-sell-by-date cereal. These days, though, there are just as many pitches selling high-end street food as there are traditional market stalls. Even a stroll of just a few metres along this road takes you past steaming grills and giant pans that send out aromas of Thai curry, Mexican chilli and slow-roasted English pork into the air. With the financial institutions of the City, the legal practices around Lincoln's Inn and a large concentration of offices in Holborn just around the corner, there are huge numbers of hungry workers to feed at lunchtime. Just like the traders that occupied this spot in the early 18th century, these stallholders are simply meeting a demand.

● Return to High Holborn and catch the eastbound **8** or **242** from the **Holborn Circus/Fetter Lane** stop. Both buses take you back into the old City of London, where the capital's original markets were held. Though the buildings may now be gleaming and futuristic, the narrow streets and lanes on which they stand are as medieval as the Black Death. Look out for the street names as you pass. Names such as Ironmonger Lane, Milk Street and Poultry reveal exactly what was sold on those particular roads more than 500 years ago.

● Get off the bus at the **Liverpool Street Station** stop and cross the road to the identically named stop on the other side. From here, catch the southbound **35**, **47**, **48**, **149** or **344** down to the **Fenchurch Street** stop and walk back up the road to **Leadenhall Market**. This glorious temple to Victoriana – designed by Sir Horace Jones, who was also responsible for Smithfield Market – features in the Harry Potter films, and it certainly has a more rarified air than bustling Leather Lane. Stalls are set up in the centre of the market until early afternoon. But even if they've been dismantled by the time you get there, the businesses lining the aisles are equally interesting. Celebrate the end of your journey with a glass of wine on the forecourt of Cheese, just inside the market entrance at number 4, and enjoy the glorious architecture around you before heading back up to Liverpool Street tube.

To download this journey to your Smartphone, scan the QR code (right)

Selfridges
Holles Street
Grays
Antiques Market
Wardour Street
Berwick
Street Market
Brownlow Street
Leather Lane Market
London
Silver Vaults
Holborn Circus/
Fetter Lane
Farringdon tube
City Thameslink Station
Smithfield Market
Liverpool Street Station
Leadenhall Market
Fenchurch Street

India House, Aldwych

18. odyssey of oddities

It's a strange place, is London. With its millions of citizens and the liberating anonymity that brings, it's no surprise people let themselves go a little bit more inside the M25. There's a lot going on – and not all of it wholesome – behind the touristy face the city presents to the world. Weirdness and eccentricity have always existed here, and London is the backdrop to many a subculture, sect or business that simply couldn't exist anywhere else. In which other British city could you experience a world of flamboyant aristocrats, Soviet spies, cloistered convents and circus freaks, all within the same couple of square miles? And the landscape of the capital can be equally odd – its buildings reflecting the outmoded attitudes and passing fads of a city that constantly updates and evolves. Dig a little deeper into London and you'll find nothing is quite as you'd expect.

Start point: Euston tube
End point: Edgware Road tube
Duration: 5 hours

● Come out of **Euston**'s main entrance, cross the main road and catch the southbound **10, 73** or **390** from the **Euston Station** stop. Get off the bus at the **University College Hospital** stop and walk back a few metres to the main gates of University College London. Bear right, then go through the door labelled South Cloisters in the far-right corner of the courtyard. You will find yourself face to face with a man who has been dead for nearly 200 years. According to his wishes, **Jeremy Bentham**, a 19th-century philosopher and social reformer, was dissected, stuffed and mummified after his death in 1832. Dressed in period clothes and seated on a chair, his body was then placed in a cabinet that has been looked after by University College since 1850. It is not Bentham's real head you are looking at, though. The original was placed in a safe after its mummified features developed a rather chilling appearance – and a few too many students 'borrowed' it to scare girls with at parties.

● Return to the **University College Hospital** bus stop and catch the southbound **390**. This bus takes you past **James Smith & Sons** on the corner of New Oxford Street – which has survived for 180 years despite selling nothing but umbrellas – before heading along Oxford Street. Just after the bus rounds Marble Arch, look to the right for **Tyburn Convent.** This cloistered community of Catholic nuns has been carrying out a continuous prayer vigil for the souls of those martyred at Tyburn gallows – sited on what's now a traffic island between Marble Arch and Edgware Road – since 1901. The nuns never go out and their community is an almost medieval presence within metres of Europe's busiest shopping street.

● Keep looking to the right and you will catch a glimpse of London's narrowest house at **10 Hyde Park Place.** Now part of Tyburn Convent, the house – which is the third door along from the nunnery's main entrance – is less than a metre wide, and incorporates just a downstairs corridor and tiny upstairs bedroom. It's thought it was built in the early 19th century with the specific purpose of preventing bodysnatchers from getting to the graveyard behind.

● Get off the bus at the **Victoria Gate** stop and continue walking along Bayswater Road. Sandwiched between the park railings and the lodge on the far side of the gate, you can glimpse London's only dedicated **pet graveyard**. Following the 1881 burial of Cherry – a terrier that belonged to friends of the gatekeeper – the site became *the* fashionable place for Bayswater residents to inter their pets. It now houses more than 300 graves.

● Cross the road and catch the southbound **148** from the **Victoria Gate** stop. This bus rounds Hyde Park and heads past Buckingham Palace gardens and Victoria Station before crossing Westminster Bridge. Look to the right for the arched entrance to the former **London Necropolis Railway** at number 121 Westminster Bridge Road. Between 1854 and 1941, this terminal was the starting point for trains that carried London's dead out to Surrey for burial, and the station housed several waiting rooms – divided, of course, according to social class – specifically for mourners.

● Stay on the bus till the **Larcom Street** stop, just beyond Elephant & Castle, then get off and go into the tiny **Cuming Museum** – located directly behind the bus stop. Little more than a couple of rooms showcasing the eclectic personal collection of a wealthy local family, the museum is worth visiting for its bizarre exhibits. In the same case, you'll see a twisted elephant tusk alongside a skinned cat and a cow's heart studded with nails. There's a stuffed bear in a box on the floor and a whole area dedicated to one family member's obsession with forgeries. Thoroughly odd yet lots of fun, it is only open from Tuesday to Saturday each week. Admission is free.

● Return to the **Larcom Road** stop and catch the southbound **12, 35, 40, 45, 68, 148, 171, 176** or **468** down to **Camberwell Road/Albany Road**. Cross the road and catch the northbound **42** from the identically named stop up through Walworth and over Tower Bridge to the **Liverpool Street Station** stop. Get off the bus and bear left onto the upper level of the station concourse. Continue around the walkway until you exit the station by the junction of Liverpool Street and Old Broad Street. Walk straight down Old Broad Street and look left for one of London's most incongruous buildings – an ornate **Turkish bathhouse**, gilded with stunning Islamic-style flourishes, which is surrounded by 1970s office blocks. Built in 1895 to satisfy a fin-de-siècle penchant for steam baths, the bathhouse became a Turkish restaurant in the early 1970s. And when property developers began turning this area into the high-rise district it is today, the owners refused to sell for les

Turkish bathhouse,
Old Broad Street

than £1 million – a staggering amount at the time. As a result, the bathhouse was left alone and blocks were built around it. In recent times, it has been a cocktail bar.

● At the bottom of Old Broad Street, cross the road, bear left and catch the westbound **8** from the **Old Broad Street** stop. Take this bus to **St Paul's Station,** then continue along Newgate Street before turning right up King Edward Street. Walk up the road for a couple of minutes then turn right into **Postman's Park** – so-named because of its proximity to the former headquarters of the General Post Office. Walk through the park and you will see the **Memorial to Heroic Self-Sacrifice** on your left. This unassuming monument, installed in 1900, commemorates the deaths of those who lost their lives in saving others in a series of beautifully decorated ceramic tiles. These briefly outline the sacrifices made in a brisk yet poignant tone that is undeniaby moving. Though most plaques date from the late 19th and early 20th centuries, one records a death as recently as 2007.

● Return to the **St Paul's Station** stop and catch the westbound **8, 25, 242** or **521.** Get off the bus at **Brownlow Street,** continue up High Holborn and turn left into the Great Turnstile alleyway. When you emerge into Lincoln's Inn Fields, walk around the park to the Royal College of Surgeons on the other side. Ask at reception to see the **Hunterian Museum,** and you will be directed to perhaps London's strangest exhibition space. Based around the personal collection of 18th-century anatomist John Hunter, the museum is an enjoyably gruesome spectacle. As well as various body parts and animals in pickling jars, it also contains the bones of some of the era's best-known 'freaks'. The 7ft 7 foot skeleton of 'Irish Giant' Charles Byrne is there, as is the skull of a man whose head grew to several times its normal size. Like the Cuming Museum, the Hunterian Museum is free to visit, and is closed on Sundays and Mondays.

● Turn left outside the Royal College of Surgeons and walk along Sardinia Street to High Holborn. Turn left and walk the short distance down to Aldwych, then bear right past the Waldorf Hotel. Look to the left as you pass **India House** – home to the High Commission of India. This is the only place in London you'll see swastikas – Eastern decorative symbols later appropriated by the Nazis – incorporated into the fabric of a building

● When you reach the bottom of Aldwych cross over the Strand and turn right. **Savoy**

Memorial to Heroic Self Sacrifice, Postman's Park

Court, the short road on the left that leads up to The Savoy hotel, is the only road in the UK on which drivers are required to drive on the right – a remnant of the days when horsedrawn carriages would have to negotiate the tight angle into the hotel entrance. Just a little further along the Strand, next to The Coal Hole pub, you'll see London's only remaining sewer-powered streetlamp, which stands at the top of **Carting Lane**. Fuelled by gas from subterranean effluent pipes, it casts a sickly glow over the Dickensian passage at night.

● Walk back along the Strand to the **Savoy Street** bus stop, and catch the westbound **9**. Once the bus turns into St James's Street, look to the right for **Pickering Place**, a perfectly preserved 16th-century alleyway next to Berry Bros & Rudd wine merchants. Get off the bus at the **Green Park Station** stop, then cross the road and turn left along Piccadilly. Turn left into Half Moon Street then, at the top, left onto Curzon Street and right into South Audley Street. After walking for a couple of minutes up this road, you'll see **Audley Square** on the right. According to double-agent Oleg Gordievsky, a colonel in the KGB during the 1960s, the lamppost outside number two was used by Soviet agents to signal to their contacts they had secrets to pass on. Chalk marks would be made on its base so spies would know to get ready to receive information. In a strange coincidence, the screenplay for the first James Bond film, *Dr No*, was written in an office at number three in 1961 and 1962 – presumably while real agents cast shifty glances around outside.

● From Audley Square, cross the road and walk straight along Tilney Street to Park Lane. Cross the road at a convenient point and turn right to catch the northbound **436** from the **Dorchester Hotel** stop. Get off at **Burwood Place**, continue walking up Edgware Road and turn right into Crawford Place. What better place to celebrate the end of your journey around London's oddities than in London's weirdest and most wonderful pub? The landlords of **The Windsor Castle** at number 27 have many passions – royalty, the theatre and C-list celebrities among them – and all are joyously celebrated on every inch of wallspace. Look out for the shrine to footballer George Best above the bar. The pub is the monthly meeting place for The Handlebar Club – a society dedicated to men with large moustaches – which seems entirely appropriate to the setting.

To download this journey to your Smartphone, scan the QR code (right).

Euston Station
Jeremy Bentham
University College Hospital
The Windsor Castle
Burwood Place
James Smith & Sons
Brownlow Street
Postman's Park
Turkish bathhouse
Liverpool Street Station
Hunterian Museum
St Paul's Station
Old Broad Street
Tyburn Convent
Victoria Gate
Pet graveyard
India House
Savoy Street
Savoy Court/ Carting Lane
Dorchester Hotel
Audley Square
Pickering Place
London Necropolis Railway
Larcom Street
Cuming Museum
Camberwell Road/ Albany Road

'Ode to the West Wind' mural, on Percy Bysshe Shelley's former home

19. book lovers' london

London is unbeatable as a literary destination. Countless novels, poems and plays have been set here, and almost all the greats of English literature have been based in the city at some point in their lives. The capital plays a crucial role in everything from Geoffrey Chaucer's 14th-century *The Canterbury Tales* – which begins as a storytelling session around the table of a Southwark inn – to 21st-century fiction such as Zadie Smith's *White Teeth*. And, thanks to the sheer scope of its geography and culture, it will continue to inspire. The literary landscape here is simply too vast for a four-hour bus journey to even begin to cover comprehensively, but this trip is an attempt to abridge it. Use the condensed version as a starting point for your own literary forays into the capital.

Start point: Westminster tube
End point: Chancery Lane tube
Duration: 4 hours

● Leave **Westminster tube** through Exit 3 and turn left. Turn left again when you reach Parliament Square and continue across the front of the Houses of Parliament, then turn right at the traffic lights. The nation's greatest writers have been interred at **Westminster Abbey** – to your left – since Geoffrey Chaucer was buried here in 1400. Though the tradition only really took off after Elizabethan poet Edmund Spenser was given a tomb in the abbey. Nowadays Poets' Corner is one of the most famous literary locations in London. Though you'll have to pay to visit it (£16 for adults at the time of writing), your entry fee allows you to visit the graves of Aphra Behn, Charles Dickens, John Dryden, Thomas Hardy and Alfred Tennyson, among others. Many more writers – including William Shakespeare – are also commemorated in the South Transept.

● Turn left upon leaving the abbey, then cross the road and catch the northbound **24** from the **Westminster Abbey** stop. The bus goes up Whitehall and St Martin's Lane to **Charing Cross Road**. This road is well-known for its second-hand and specialist bookshops, which line its right-hand side. It was the letters exchanged between the proprietor of one of these and US author Helene Hanff that formed the basis of her 1970 book *84 Charing Cross Road*. Depressingly, the premises is now a branch of Pizza Hut.

● Get off the bus at the **Denmark Street** stop, walk back down Charing Cross Road and turn right into **Old Compton Street**. In the late 19th century, Old Compton Street was at the heart of London's French quarter, and Gallic poets Paul Verlaine and Arthur Rimbaud – who lived together on nearby Great College Street – would come here to drink absinthe in the Hibernia Street Arms, which was situated at number 23.

● Continue along Old Compton Street, crossing **Frith Street** – home to essayist William Hazlitt in the early 19th century – and **Dean Street**, which is where both Karl Marx and Friedrich Engels lived in the 1850s. Dean Street is also the location of **The French House** pub, a favourite of writers Brendan Behan and John Mortimer. Dylan Thomas, another regular, once left the manuscript for his 1950s drama *Under Milk Wood* beneath a chair here.

● Turn right up Wardour Street then, after a few minutes, left into Broadwick

he French House,
Dean Street, Soho

Street. Poet William Blake was born on this road in 1757. **Blake House,** a Brutalist tower block on the corner of Broadwick Street and Marshall Street, now occupies the site of his former home. Continue straight on, passing the Spirit of Soho mural – which commemorates Blake and other great literary figures associated with the district – and turn right up Carnaby Street.

● At the top, turn right onto Great Marlborough Street. When you reach the junction with **Poland Street,** look right to see the house in which Percy Bysshe Shelley lived in 1811. The mural on the side of the building is inspired by his poem 'Ode to the West Wind'. Turn left up Poland Street – passing number 28 on the right, which is where Blake lived between 1785 and 1791.

● Cross Oxford Street, turn left and catch the eastbound **55** from the **Great Titchfield Street** stop. This passes the southern edges of **Bloomsbury** – the district in which Virginia Woolf, EM Forster and other members of the Bloomsbury Set lived and worked in the early 20th century – before heading through **Clerkenwell,** setting for Peter Ackroyd's 2003 *The Clerkenwell Tales* and George Gissing's 1889 *The Nether World*. This is also the area in which Dickens' Oliver Twist first tries his hand at pickpocketing.

● Get off the bus at **Old Street Station,** continue along the road and turn right at the roundabout. Walk down City Road and you'll see **Bunhill Fields** on the right. This was London's main non-conformist graveyard between the 17th and 19th centuries, and is the resting place for those who refused to accept the established Anglican Church. William Blake's headstone stands in the central square, just across from the tomb in which lies John Bunyan – author of *The Pilgrim's Progress*.

● Retrace your steps to City Road, cross over and turn left. Catch the southbound **21** from the **City Road/Leonard Street** stop and take it all the way to **Southwark Street.** Walk back up Borough High Street and turn right into **Talbot Yard,** which is where The Tabard Inn – the pub in which Chaucer's pilgrims gather in *The Canterbury Tales* – was situated between 1307 and 1873. A plaque on the wall of Copyprints is all that remains. Further up Borough High Street is **The George Inn,** a galleried pub that dates back to medieval times, which was frequented by both Charles Dickens and William Shakespeare – who would drop in for a

William Blake's grave, Bunhill Fields

pint after performances at the Globe Theatre, just along the South Bank.

● Turn left down Southwark Street and catch the westbound **RV1** or **381** from the **Hop Exchange** stop. Get off at **Blackfriars Bridge** and walk over the bridge. Turn right onto Queen Victoria Street, left up Black Friars Lane and right into Playhouse Yard. This leads onto **Ireland Yard**, which is where Shakespeare lived from 1613 until his death in 1616. Handy for the theatres across the river, this was a very exclusive address in the Jacobean era. Poet and playwright Ben Jonson also had a house here.

● Turn left at the end of Ireland Yard and walk up St Andrew's Hill to Carter Lane. Turn left then right up Black Friars Lane; and, when you reach Pilgrim Street, turn left then immediately right to emerge onto Ludgate Hill. Walk straight up Old Bailey to the **Old Bailey** central criminal court, which is where the three trials involving Oscar Wilde – the first the libel action he brought against the Marquis of Queensberry for calling him a 'somdomite'; the other two for charges of sodomy and gross indecency – took place in 1895. The courthouse stands on the site of the infamous Newgate Prison, which is where Daniel Defoe was imprisoned for pamphleteering in 1703. His experiences here led him to write *Moll Flanders* – the eponymous heroine of which begins her colourful life in Newgate.

● Retrace your steps to Ludgate Hill, cross the road and turn right. Catch the westbound **4**, **11**, **15**, **23**, **26**, **76** or **172** from the **City Thameslink Station/ Ludgate Circus** stop. Get off at the **Shoe Lane** stop, cross the road and turn left. Finish your journey with a drink in **Ye Olde Cheshire Cheese**, accessed via an alleyway on the right. Though the pub has been here since 1538, the current building dates from the late 17th century. And over the years it has served drinks to everyone from Oliver Goldsmith and Samuel Johnson to Charles Dickens, Alfred Tennyson and Arthur Conan-Doyle. The pub was also the meeting place of the Rhymers Club, the poetry society formed by WB Yeats in 1890 that included Oscar Wilde and Alfred Douglas among its members.

● Once you've had enough of the pub's unique literary ambience, retrace your steps to Fleet Street and turn right. Turn right up Chancery Lane then, at the top, right again for **Chancery Lane tube**.

To download this journey to your Smartphone, scan the QR code (right).

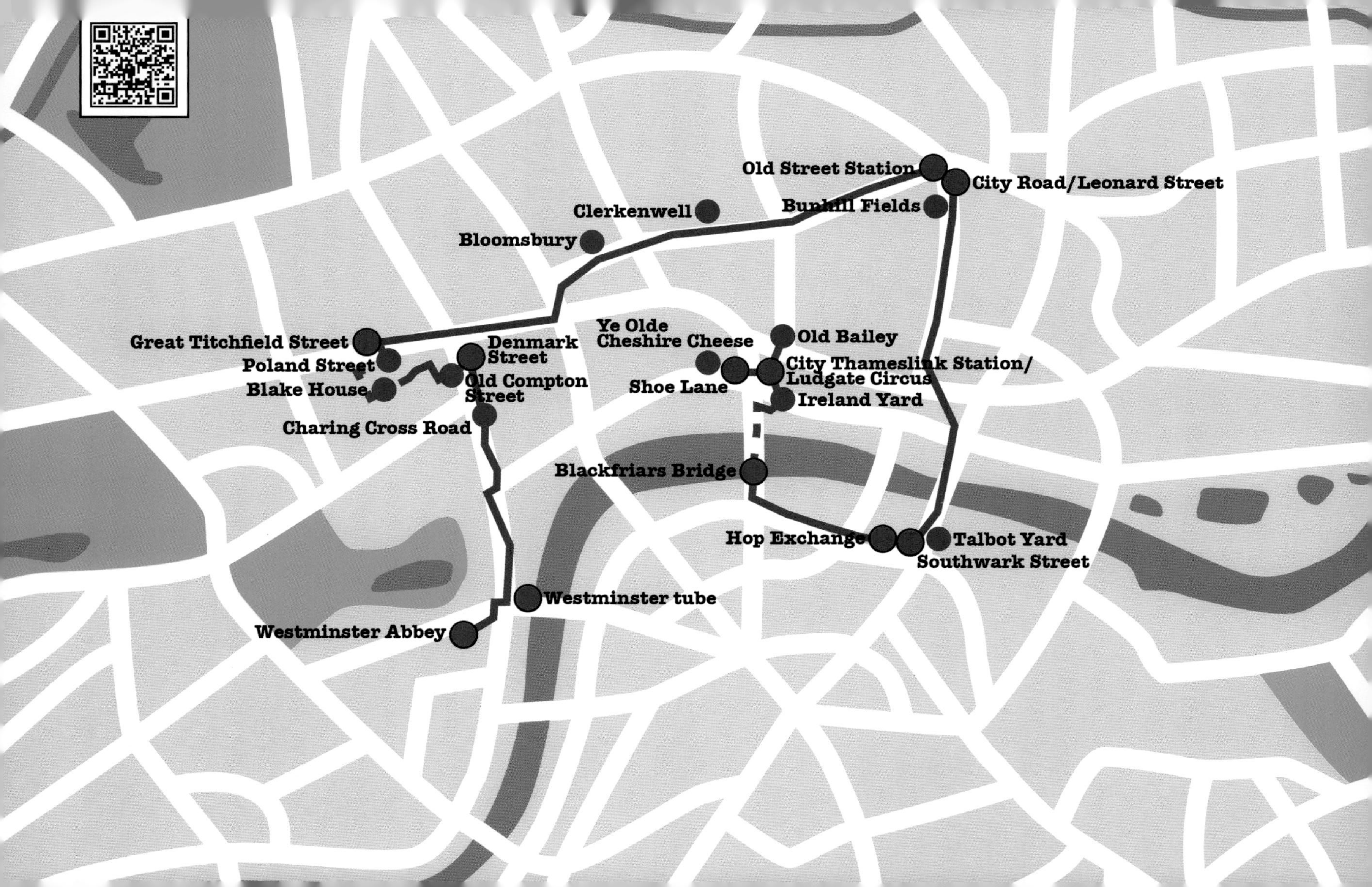
Old Street Station
City Road/Leonard Street
Bunhill Fields
Clerkenwell
Bloomsbury
Great Titchfield Street
Poland Street
Blake House
Denmark Street
Old Compton Street
Charing Cross Road
Ye Olde Cheshire Cheese
Shoe Lane
Old Bailey
City Thameslink Station/ Ludgate Circus
Ireland Yard
Blackfriars Bridge
Hop Exchange
Talbot Yard
Southwark Street
Westminster tube
Westminster Abbey

20. jewish london

The history of the Jews in London is a long and complicated one. The city's first sizeable Jewish community was established off Cheapside in the late 11th century, when refugees from French pogroms settled in the capital to boost the fledgling Norman economy. Barely 200 years later, they were gone – expelled from England by King Edward I on the back of rampant anti-semitism. For the next 350 years, Judaism was equivalent to witchcraft in the popular imagination; and when Jews did begin resettling in London, they were met with suspicion and hostility. The traditionally Jewish areas of the East End have long been abandoned in favour of more affluent northern suburbs but, as befits their status as one of the city's longest-established ethnic groups, the Jewish community has left its mark throughout the capital.

Start point: Golders Green tube
End point: Camden Town tube
Duration: 5 hours

● Exit **Golders Green tube,** turn right and walk along the path to the right of the small parade of shops. You will emerge alongside an enclosed section of road, which has **Golders Green Station** bus stop on the far side. For a brief tour of north London's most prosperous Jewish suburbs, take the **H2** from here. This bus, which begins and terminates at this stop, first heads down **Golders Green Road,** the district's main thoroughfare, upon which you'll see Jewish restaurants, kosher burger bars and beigel bakeries amid the high-street chains. Jews began settling in Golders Green and the surrounding districts in the early 20th century, when the Charing Cross, Euston and Hampstead Railway built an underground train line out to this part of northwest London – already known for its Jewish cemetery. This gave wealthy East End Jews the option of bringing up families in suburbia while still maintaining businesses close to the City.

● After turning up Hoop Lane, the bus passes **Golders Green Jewish Cemetery** on the left. Reform Jews (those who believe in modern and liberal interpretations of the Torah and Jewish traditions) are buried on western side. The eastern side of the cemetery is reserved for orthodox Sephardic Jews (those who can trace their ancestry back to 15th-century Jewish communities in Spain and Portugal), who are buried in flat graves with their feet pointing towards Jerusalem. The cemetery, which opened in 1895, is the final resting place of cellist Jacqueline du Pré, who converted to Judaism in 1967.

● **Golders Green Crematorium,** directly opposite the cemetery, was opened in 1902. Despite being totally secular, it is where many notable British-based Jews – including Sigmund Freud, Amy Winehouse and Mark Bolan – have chosen to be cremated. The ashes of Gentiles Enid Blyton, Keith Moon and Bram Stoker, among others, are scattered in beautifully landscaped gardens behind.

● The remainder of the bus journey is spent meandering around Hampstead Garden Suburb. With its neat housing, ornamental gardens and somewhat twee open spaces, this early 20th-century piece of idealistic urban planning is more Stepford than Sephardic. Its large Jewish population, though, is a reminder of how far London's Jews have come since the days in which they were based in the poverty-stricken slums of the East

End. These streets have some of the highest property prices in the capital, and the people who live here are at the top of the capital's economic tree.

● When the bus returns to the **Golders Green Station** stop, get off and walk back to the tube station entrance. Catch the southbound **13** from the bus station in front of the forecourt and take it all the way into central London. Get off at the **Aldwych/Drury Lane** terminus, continue walking around Aldwych and along Fleet Street, then turn left up Chancery Lane. The Maughan Library, on your right, is built on the site of the medieval **Domus Conversorum** (House of the Converts), which was established in 1253 to encourage Jews to convert to Christianity. When King Edward I formally expelled all Jews from England in 1290, conversion became the only way to remain in the country. But as acknowledging Christ meant all property and assets had to be forfeited to the state, those who did decide to stay were forced to take up residence here and live a life of destitution. Unsurprisingly, only a very small number of Jews took this deal; most preferred to leave the country or practice their religion in secret.

● Carry on walking up Chancery Lane, turn left at the top and cross the road to the **Brownlow Street** stop. Catch the eastbound **25**, which heads down High Holborn and past Hatton Garden on the left. London's diamond and jewellery trade, centred around this street since medieval times, has been dominated by Orthodox Jews since Oliver Cromwell readmitted Judaism to England in 1656. The Lord Protector was desperate to attract Jewish diamond dealers from Antwerp to London to boost an ailing economy and generate lucrative taxes.

● When the bus goes along Cheapside and Poultry, look to the left for **Old Jewry**, which marks the entrance to London's original Jewish ghetto – that stretched as far as St Giles Without Cripplegate in the north to Poultry in the south. William the Conqueror installed survivors of the Rouen pogrom here in 1096 as he needed money-lenders to help make his new kingdom more prosperous (the medieval Church forbade Christians from lending money at interest). Even though this trade was imposed on the Jewish community, the riches it brought led to Jews being resented – especially in times of hardship – and this often spilled over into anti-semitic violence. Old Jewry was the scene of a brutal pogrom in 1189, when Londoners – acting on a rumour that King Richard I had ordered a massacre of the

Jewish newspaper logo,
Whitechapel Road

Jews – set fire to Jewish houses, and killed those fleeing the flames.

● Get off the bus at the **St Katherine Cree** stop, and continue along Leadenhall Street and St Botolph Street. Turn left into Duke's Place and follow the road along until it becomes Bevis Marks. **Bevis Marks Synagogue**, on the left, was built by London's new Sephardic community in 1701. It is the oldest synagogue in the UK. The spiritual and administrative heart of Judaism in the English-speaking world for centuries, it houses a stunning Renaissance-style oak ark that holds the Torah scrolls.

● Walk back down Bevis Marks and Duke's Place, and turn left into St Botolph Street. Cross Houndsditch and turn left up Middlesex Street, then right into **Goulston Street**. It was in the doorway to number 108 that the Goulston Street graffito – which read 'the Juwes [sic] are the men that will not be blamed for nothing' – was found in 1888, scrawled above a piece of bloodstained apron belonging to Jack the Ripper's fourth victim Catherine Eddowes. As anti-semitic feeling was running high in the East End, in part due to suspicions that local Jewish cobbler John Pizer was responsible for the Whitechapel murders, police washed away the writing almost immediately. Detectives were divided over whether the graffito had anything to do with the case. While some felt it was a message from the murderer that required greater interpretation, others saw it as just another expression of East End anti-Jewish feeling that happened to be where the criminal had flung the incriminating cloth.

● Return to Middlesex Street, turn right and walk up to Cobb Street. Turn right here, left up Bell Street and right into **Brune Street**. The Soup Kitchen for the Jewish Poor, on the left, was established in 1854 to feed impoverished Russian Jews who flocked into London at this time to escape pogroms in the east. Whitechapel and Spitalfields were desperately poor areas in the 19th century, and this building is a potent reminder that Jews were at the very bottom of the pile.

● Retrace your steps to Middlesex Street then turn right and follow the road along Petticoat Lane Market onto Bishopsgate. Cross the road, turn left and catch the northbound **8** from the **Liverpool Street Station** stop. Get off at the **Brick Lane** stop, carry on walking along Bethnal Green Road and turn right down Brick Lane. Though this road is now known for its Bangladeshi population, it used to be the heart of Jewish Spitalfields. You'll see remnants of this immediately to the right –

Beigel bakery, Brick Lane

the Brick Lane Beigel Bake and Britain's First & Best Beigel Shop, established in 1855, form a tiny Jewish enclave amid the curry houses and sari shops of Banglatown.

● Continue down Brick Lane, passing the London Jamme Masjid mosque that occupies the former Spitalfields Great Synagogue. Walk all the way down to Whitechapel Road and turn right to see the wonderfully ornate star of David above the door of Albert's men's outfitters at number 88. Part of the logo for a Jewish newspaper that operated from these premises in the 1920s, it remained on the wall after the publication closed and the Jewish community left the East End behind.

● Turn around and walk back up Whitechapel Road to the **Osborn Street** bus stop. Catch the northbound **254**, which takes you up through Hackney and Clapton to **Stamford Hill** – home to the largest Orthodox Jewish community outside of Israel and the US. Here you will see Ashkenazi Jews (descended from the medieval Jewish communities around the River Rhine in Germany) in the traditional dress of fur hats, black coats and white stockings. Many businesses are run by and cater to the local Jewish population, and several stores specialise in disposable cooking, eating and food storage implements, as the predominantly Hasidic population are forbidden from cooking and washing-up on the Sabbath. The area welcomed its first Jewish residents in the 1880s, as Ashkenazi Jews sought to escape the East End slums. Once the Union of Orthodox Hebrew Congregations was established in Stamford Hill in 1926 with the aim of protecting traditional Judaism, the area became a magnet for Orthodox and Hasidic families.

● Get off the bus at the **Stamford Hill Broadway** stop and catch the westbound **253** from the same stop. This bus takes you to Camden Town – home of the **Jewish Museum London**, dedicated to the British-Jewish experience. Several hands-on exhibits, including a recreation of a Jewish East End tailor's shop and a Yiddish karaoke booth, make the museum as fun an experience as an educational one; and exhibitions on British-Jewish life and the impact of the Holocaust are both enlightening and moving. To get to the museum, get off the 253 at the **Camden Town Station** stop and walk back to Camden Road. Turn right, cross at the lights and walk up Parkway, then turn left onto Albert Street. The museum is on the right.

To download this journey to your Smartphone, scan the QR code (right).

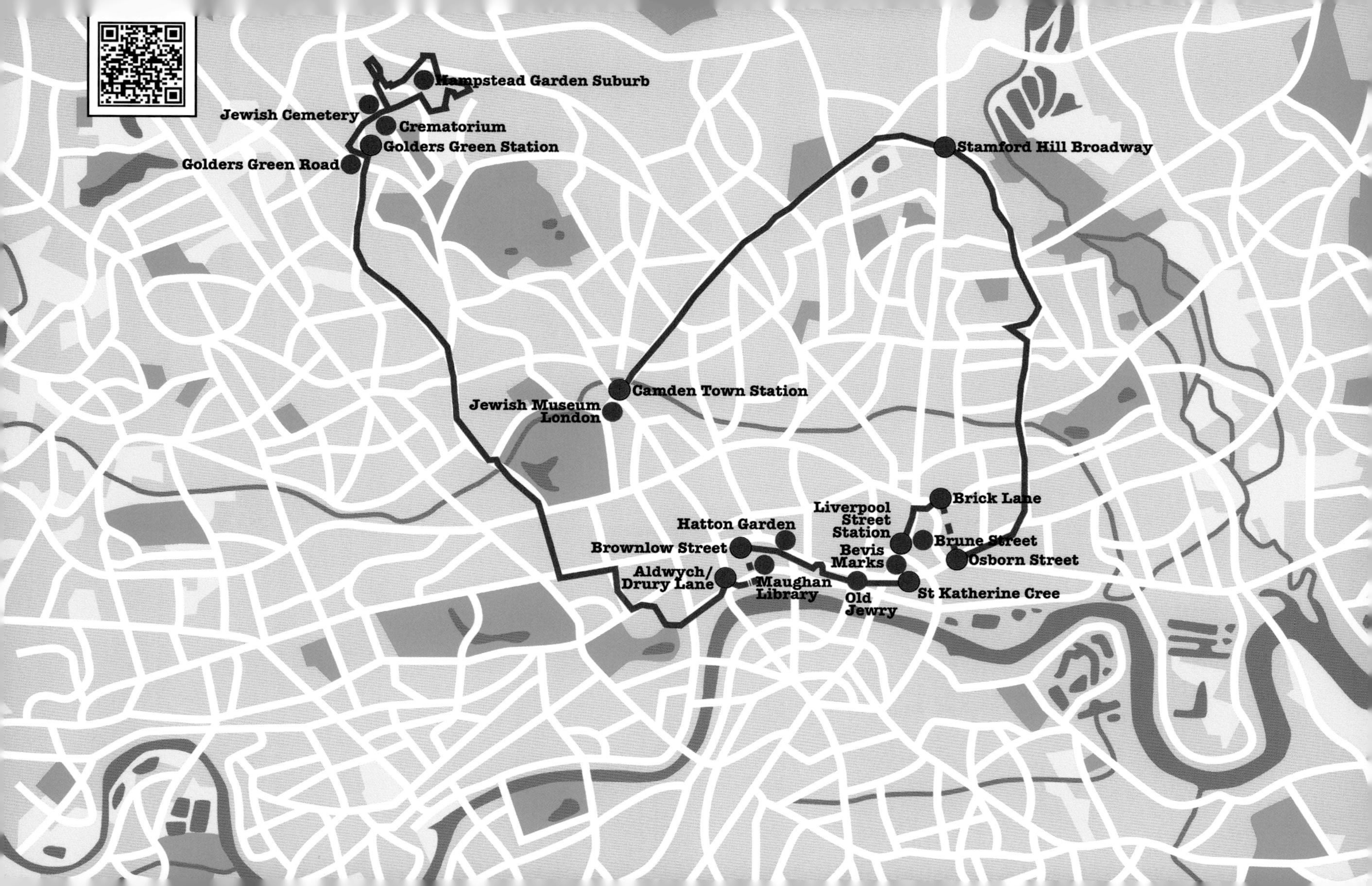
Hampstead Garden Suburb
Jewish Cemetery
Crematorium
Golders Green Station
Golders Green Road
Stamford Hill Broadway
Camden Town Station
Jewish Museum London
Brick Lane
Liverpool Street Station
Hatton Garden
Brune Street
Bevis Marks
Brownlow Street
Osborn Street
Aldwych/ Drury Lane
Maughan Library
Old Jewry
St Katherine Cree

South Molton Street

21. fashion trips

Milan for business, Paris for style, New York for wearability. And London? The city has been the home of cutting-edge fashion since Biba's hedonistic heyday in the 1960s and – thanks to the talent emerging each year from its renowned fashion schools – it keeps its perfectly accessorised finger firmly on fashion's pulse. The world's style capital continues to evolve, though; and on this journey, as you ponder the influence of Browns, Savile Row and Zandra Rhodes on the London look, you'll see the city's various style tribes in all their resplendent glory. As you pass the beautifully coiffured citizens of the King's Road and the beyond-cool media types in Soho, it's tempting to think of the city as one giant catwalk.

49
GOLFINO
Sportswear
GOLFINO

Start point: Sloane Square tube
End point: London Bridge tube
Duration: 4.5 hours

● Come out of **Sloane Square tube,** turn left and catch the westbound **22** from the **Sloane Square Station** stop. This bus heads down the famous **King's Road**, which was one of London's earliest fashion destinations. This is where Mary Quant – inventor of the miniskirt – had her boutique Bazaar at 138A, a store that was instrumental in bringing the new innovative British fashion movement to the world's attention in the 1960s.

● The fashion industry, though, is about more than the designers and the clothes they make. Equally prominent in the public consciousness are the models who showcase the designs, and who can make or break a label. Jubilee Place, also on the right-hand side of King's Road, is the home of the **Storm Modelling Agency,** which has looked after the careers of some of the world's most famous models – including Carla Bruni, Cindy Crawford, Eva Herzigova and Kate Moss.

● Look out for number 430 on the right. Now designer Vivienne Westwood's World's End store, this was where Westwood and her boyfriend Malcolm McLaren had their infamous boutique **SEX** in the mid-1970s. Selling bondage gear and seditious T-shirts, the shop was instrumental in bringing punk fashion into the mainstream. Helped no end, of course, by the fact that The Sex Pistols, the band McLaren managed – which included the shop's Saturday boy Glen Matlock on bass – happened to be the most notorious punk-rock band in the world.

● Get off the bus at the **Edith Grove/ World's End** stop, walk back up King's Road and turn right into Beaufort Street. Catch the northbound **49** from the **Beaufort Street/King's Road** stop and get off at the **South Kensington Station/ Brompton Road** stop. Either take the tunnel that leads from the tube station concourse or follow signs to the **Victoria & Albert Museum.** Once you're in the museum (admission is free), head straight for the Fashion Galleries. Showcasing European fashions, fabrics and accessories from the mid-18th century to the present day, these rooms have long been a source of inspiration for British designers. Even if you're not looking to reinvent the epaulette they are a fascinating insight into an ever-changing sartorial world.

● Upon leaving the museum, catch the eastbound **74** from the **Victoria & Alber**

Liberty, Great Marlborough Street

Museum stop just outside its main entrance on Cromwell Gardens. The bus heads up Knightsbridge towards Hyde Park, passing this district's two temples to fashion – **Harrod's** and **Harvey Nichols**, both of which are renowned for their superb seasonal collections. Get off the bus at the **Portman Street/Selfridges** stop to visit **Selfridges**, another of the city's great department stores – famed for its innovative window displays, often put together in conjunction with some of the world's greatest fashion designers.

● When you've finished browsing through the hundreds of in-store outlets, exit onto Oxford Street and catch the eastbound **6** from the **Selfridges** stop in front of the building. Look right as you approach Bond Street tube to see boutique-lined **South Molton Street** – where the city's discerning shoppers bring their credit cards. Browns at number 27 on the right has, over the past 40 years, been perhaps the most influential in bringing cutting-edge British design to a wider audience. John Galliano, Alexander McQueen and Hussein Chalayan all owe their careers to this store and its buyers' eye for talent.

● The bus then goes across the top of **New Bond Street** on the right. The city's main fashion thoroughfare, this road has been associated with high-end luxury since the 18th century. Lined with branches of the major international fashion houses – from Armani to Zegna – it is a seriously glitzy destination, and the first port of call for Hollywood A-listers when they're in town. The street is also where hairdresser Vidal Sassoon had his salon in the 1960s – and it was here that he created the five-point bob, the haircut that defined the Swinging London look.

● When the bus reaches Oxford Circus tube, look to the left for a glimpse of **The London College of Fashion** – which is situated behind the enormous H&M store. Though this college doesn't quite have the pedigree of fellow London establishments Goldsmiths or Central St Martins in churning out world-beating design talent, it still has an impressive list of alumni – especially from its shoe-design faculty. Patrick Cox, Jimmy Choo and Emma Hope all studied here.

● Once the bus turns down Regent Street get off at the **Conduit Street/Hamleys Toy Store** stop and cross the road. Bear right down New Burlington Street and turn right onto **Savile Row,** the centre of men's tailoring in the UK. At the top of the road turn left and then immediately right onto St George Street. When you reach Hanover

ashion & Textile Museum,
ermondsey Street

Square, turn right and you'll find yourself in front of **Vogue House** – the home of Condé Nast UK, where fashion bibles *Vogue* and *Tatler* are put together each month. Along with *Harpers Bazaar*, produced on the other side of Regent Street on Broadwick Street, these magazines are perhaps the most influential mouthpieces of the high-fashion world.

● Walk across the front of Vogue House and continue along Hanover Street, then cross Regent Street and walk down Great Marlborough Street. Look right for the iconic timbered facade of **Liberty**, every fashionista's favourite London department store due to its expertly curated collections and impeccable good taste. Turn right immediately after Liberty and walk down **Carnaby Street**, which was famously the heartbeat of London's Swinging Sixties fashion scene, lampooned by The Kinks in their 1966 song *Dedicated Follower of Fashion*.

● At the bottom of Carnaby Street, bear left and continue walking down Upper James Street, through Golden Square, and down Lower James Street and Sherwood Street until you reach Piccadilly Circus tube. Turn right up Regent Street and catch the southbound **139** from the **Piccadilly Circus** stop. When the bus turns right and heads down Haymarket, look to the right for **Jermyn Street**, another centre of men's tailoring known for the quality of its handmade shirts. Get off the bus at the **Southampton Street** stop and walk along the Strand to **Somerset House** – venue for all the showpiece events in the biannual London Fashion Week.

● Catch the southbound **188** from the **Aldwych/Somerset House** stop and take it all the way to the **Abbey Street** stop. Continue walking up Tower Bridge Road and turn left onto Tanner Street. Turn right up Bermondsey Street and walk up to the **Fashion & Textile Museum,** established by British designer Zandra Rhodes in 2003. The museum offers three major exhibitions each year on seminal fashion and textile design movements, as well as a fascinating permanent collection that includes 3,000 original garments donated by Rhodes herself.

● To get to the nearest tube, turn right upon leaving the museum. At the top of Bermondsey Street, turn left onto St Thomas Street and walk straight on to Borough High Street. Turn left here for **London Bridge tube.**

To download this journey to your Smartphone, scan the QR code (right)

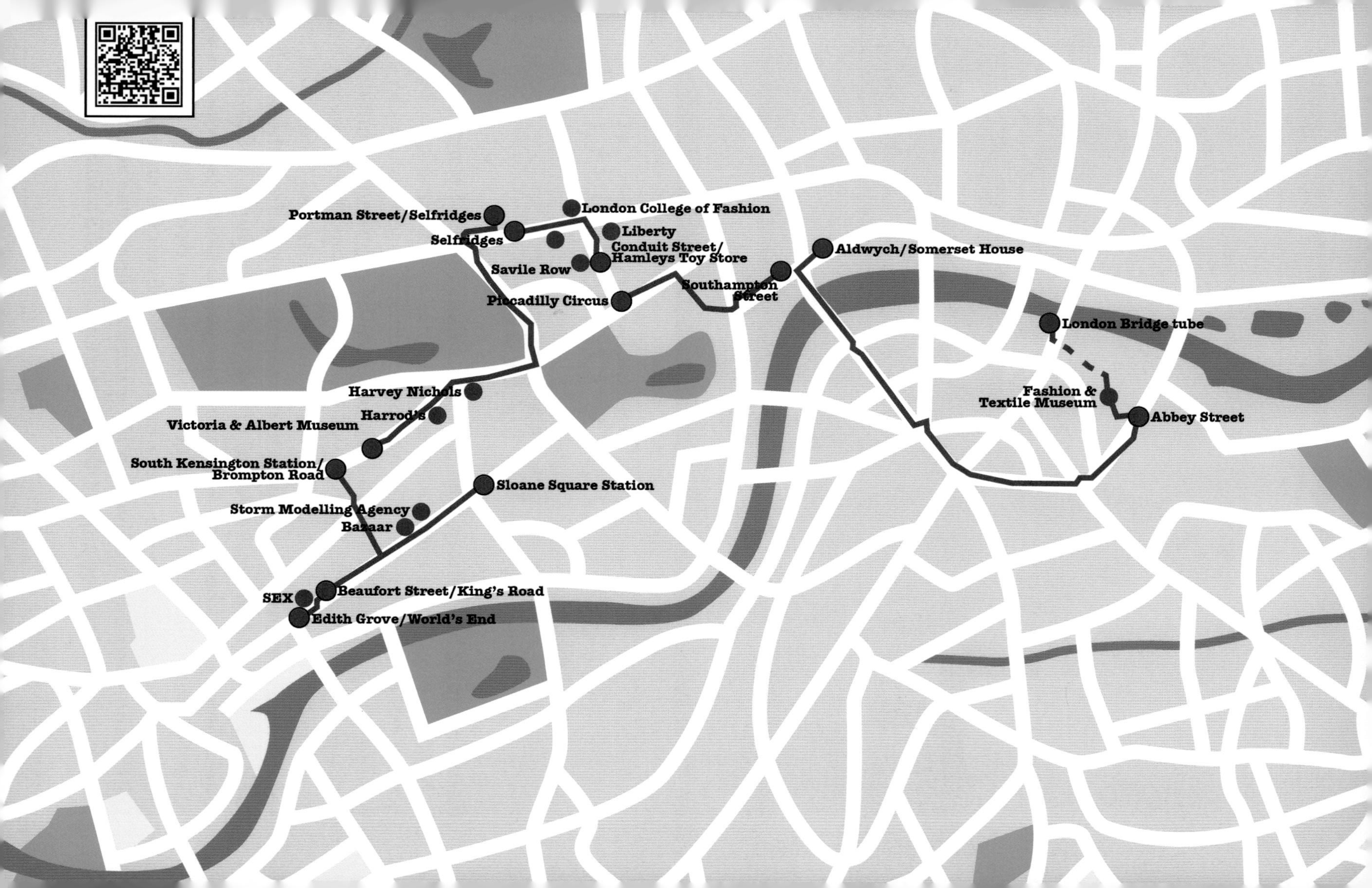
London College of Fashion
Portman Street/Selfridges
Liberty
Selfridges
Conduit Street/
Hamleys Toy Store
Aldwych/Somerset House
Savile Row
Southampton
Street
Piccadilly Circus
London Bridge tube
Harvey Nichols
Fashion &
Textile Museum
Abbey Street
Harrod's
Victoria & Albert Museum
South Kensington Station/
Brompton Road
Sloane Square Station
Storm Modelling Agency
Bazaar
Beaufort Street/King's Road
SEX
Edith Grove/World's End

The Dublin Castle, Camden Town

22. rock around the block

New York may have more attitude, Paris strikes more of a pose and Rio is better at moving its hips, but when it comes to rock and pop, London has all the best tunes. The city has been immortalised in song by generations of musicians and inspired countless young wannabes to pick up an instrument in the hope of becoming a star. It has always had its ear to the ground when it comes to fresh sounds and ideas, and its cafés and clubs have given birth to numerous scenes, from the wartime jazz of Soho and the folk revival of the Sixties to punk, 1980s dance music, Britpop and beyond. As for the bus you're sitting on, well, it's an essential part of the city's musical life: sitting top deck after a late-night gig is a rite of passage for every music lover. Even the squeaky clean Cliff Richard wouldn't be where he is today without the red double-decker, which rumbled across the big screen in 1963's *Summer Holiday*.

Start point: Westbourne Park tube
End point: Highbury & Islington tube
Duration: 3.5 hours

● Come out of the tube station, turn right and cross over the road to catch the southbound **328** from the **Westbourne Park Station** stop. After the bus stops at St Stephen's Gardens on Chepstow Road, it passes **Talbot Road** – where Geoff Travis set up his independent **Rough Trade** shop and record label in 1978, home to punky reggae bands and, later, The Smiths – on the right. **Stiff Records**, which fostered Elvis Costello, The Damned, The Pogues and Ian Dury, had its headquarters on Alexander Street, at the other end of Talbot Road. This once down-at-heel area has enjoyed a bohemian reputation since the 1950s, when West Indian émigrés moved here; by the 1960s it was a counterculture melting pot: Mick Jagger's trippy 1968 film *Performance* was partly filmed in a stucco-fronted house on the corner of Talbot Road and Powys Square. And at 103 Talbot Road is The Globe, a Caribbean basement café that has dished up rice and peas to Bob Marley, Jimi Hendrix and Van Morrison.

● One of the area's most flamboyant musical landmarks is the Notting Hill Carnival, whose floats and feather-and-sequin-covered dancers parade down Chepstow Road each August Bank Holiday. Held in Notting Hill since 1965, it now attracts around a million people and a certain amount of notoriety: a disturbance during the 1976 Carnival inspired Joe Strummer to write The Clash's *White Riot*. Walk the streets of Notting Hill in the mid-1970s and you would have heard a soundtrack of Junior Murvin, The Upsetters, Max Romeo and Big Youth; reggae's basslines reverberated through the music of the 1970s and had a major influence on punk bands such as The Clash, who responded with songs such as *White Man in Hammersmith Palais* and *Guns of Brixton*.

● As the bus rolls down Pembridge Road and past numerous souvenir shops, see how many T-shirts you can see bearing the Rolling Stones' iconic 'lips and tongue' image, first used on the *Sticky Fingers* album. You'll then turn left onto **Notting Hill Gate**, where a youthful Richard Branson opened his third Virgin Records shop at number 130 (now a Holland & Barrett, just visible to the right as the bus turns onto Notting Hill Gate). Customers were given scatter cushions and free veggie food; in 1972 the Virgin Records label was founded in an upstairs office. First signing? Mike Oldfield. Branson bought him a set of tubular bells for £20.

● After turning off Kensington High Street, the 328 passes **Logan Place** on the right before it reaches Earl's Court. Queen frontman Freddie Mercury had his home at number 1, the Garden Lodge, and he died here in 1991. The green door is covered with graffiti from fans who make a pilgrimage here. Out of sight, further up the High Street, was Kensington Market, closed in 2000, where every band and singer worth their salt, from The Kinks and Roxy Music to Robbie Williams, would go for fashion inspiration; in the mid-1970s, you might have bought some vintage clothes from Freddie Mercury and Roger Taylor, who ran a stall there.

● When the bus crosses Old Brompton Road, look out for **The Troubadour Club** to the right on the far side. This original 1950s coffee house was a major player in the folk revival of the 1960s: Paul Simon, Sandy Denny, Davey Graham and Bert Jansch all played here, as well as Bob Dylan, who appeared under the name Blind Boy Grunt. If you fancy stopping here for lunch, order a bowl of the herb-and-tomato pasta, which has been on the menu for half a century and has sustained countless singer-songwriters.

● Get off the bus at the **Hobury Street/ World's End** stop. Continue walking up King's Road, pausing at number 430 on the left – which is where Malcolm MacLaren and Vivienne Westwood ran a cutting-edge fashion boutique which, by 1974, was named **SEX** in large pink letters (with the tagline 'Rubber wear for the office'). In 1980, Westwood renamed the shop World's End, the name it bears today. The huge clock built into its façade is set to spin backwards, counting down to the end of the world. It was here that all four members of the Sex Pistols would hang out, although it was at number 354, in a pub called the Roebuck (now a private-hire venue) that John Lydon was formally introduced to the others and auditioned by singing along to Alice Cooper's *(I'm) Eighteen* on the jukebox.

● Catch the eastbound **22** from the **Beaufort Street** stop on King's Road and take it all the way to the **Hyde Park Corner Station** stop. If it's sunny, you may want to stretch your legs in **Hyde Park**, London's largest and, since 1968, the setting for numerous outdoor performances. Pink Floyd started it all during the Midsummer High Weekend in

Cecil Sharp House,
Primrose Hill

June 1968, when the opening bars of *Let There Be More Light* ushered in an era of free concerts. The most famous was the Rolling Stones' in 1969, which took place two days after Brian Jones' death. The band played to an estimated 250,000 people; Mick Jagger recited Shelley in tribute to his late guitarist and released dozens of white butterflies into the air – a gesture repeated (with doves) 36 years later by U2 at the Live 8 charity concert.

● Catch the eastbound **14** from the same stop. As this heads up Shaftesbury Avenue from Piccadilly Circus, you should have time to look right down Wardour Street. The blue O'Neill's pub on the right occupies a building that in the 1960s housed a basement jazz and R&B joint called the **Flamingo Club**, in which Georgie Fame had a residency and where Hendrix and the Who jammed on stage. Upstairs was the **Whisky A Go Go** club – later known as the WAG club – which in the 1980s saw Sade and The Pogues playing some of their first gigs, and hip-hop pioneer Grandmaster Flash make his UK debut on the wheels of steel.

● On the other side of Wardour Street (to the left) is where the **Marquee Club** was located at number 90 – the building still has a musical connection, as Cuban bands often play at downstairs restaurant Floridita. This famous club hosted early gigs by The Who, Led Zeppelin, The Jimi Hendrix Experience and Pink Floyd in the late 1960s and early 1970s. If you get off the bus, look for the blue plaque honouring Keith Moon. Thanks to performances by Def Leppard and Iron Maiden, it was at the forefront of the new wave of heavy metal in the early 1980s, and was famous for its 'secret' gigs – Prince, the Jam, Genesis and Metallica all played here under pseudonyms.

● The bus then almost immediately passes the end of Dean Street – home to nightclub and New Romantic epicentre **Billy's** – on the left. It then passes Frith Street (where world-famous jazz venue **Ronnie Scott's** has been located since 1965, and where Jimi Hendrix played his last live gig) and Greek Street, where folk club **Les Cousins** – haunt of John Martyn, Bert Jansch, Al Stewart and all the major figures of the 1960s folk revival – was situated at number 49. Both roads can be seen on the left.

● The bus then turns up Charing Cross Road, passing **Denmark Street** on the right. Known as England's Tin Pan Alley,

Denmark Street

this is the city's ultimate music street. 'Just open your ears and follow your nose, 'cos the street is shaken' from the tapping of toes', according to a song by The Kinks. *Melody Maker* was first published here in 1926 (at number 19), followed by the *NME* (at number 5) in 1952 (which produced the first singles and album chart). Look out for the Regent Sounds Studio sign at number 4 (now a guitar shop): this is where The Rolling Stones recorded their first album in 1964, and where both Hendrix and Donovan made their first recordings. David Bowie used to live in a camper van that he parked on the street here in order to be close to the studio, and drank tea at number 9, the Mod-friendly Giaconda Café, where he met his first backing band, the Lower 3rd. Bob Marley bought his first guitar on Denmark Street, and the Sex Pistols lived above the shop at number 6 while Elton John wrote *Your Song* at number 20 – where he worked as an office boy in 1970. These days, you can buy everything from guitar strings and banjos to synths and amps, but the only place you can hear live music is the tiny **12 Bar Club**, which has seen intimate gigs by Martha Wainwright, the Libertines and Jeff Buckley. Get off the bus at the **Tottenham Court Road Station** stop, walk back to the junction and turn right into Oxford Street.

● Cross the road and catch the westbound **7** from the **Oxford Street/Soho Street** stop. Look out for the **100 Club** (at 100 Oxford Street) on the right. During World War II, this was a jazz venue that attracted jitterbugging American GIs and musicians such as Glenn Miller and Benny Goodman. Three decades later, it reverberated to a different sound, when it was a mecca for punk fans – on 20 September 1976 it hosted the famous 100 Club Punk Special, which helped launch the careers of the Sex Pistols, The Clash, Buzzcocks, Siouxsie and the Banshees, and the Stranglers. It was due to close in 2010 but, thanks to a charity gig by Paul McCartney, raised enough funds to continue. At the other end of Oxford Street, the tiny alleyway opposite Selfridges leads to **Balderton Street**, where auditions for The Spice Girls were held at number 16 in 1994 – the five girls all replied to an advert in *The Stage*, which asked: 'RU 18–23 with the ability to sing/dance? RU streetwise, outgoing, ambitious and dedicated?' If you really, really want, get off the bus at the **Marble Arch Station** stop.

● Cross Oxford Street, turn right and then left up Portman Street. Catch the

Live music advertised at The Dublin Castle, Camden Town

northbound **274** from the **Portman Street/Selfridges** stop. As it goes down Gloucester Place, you may want to hum the saxophone solo from Gerry Rafferty's *Baker Street*, which runs parallel. The bus passes the pastel-coloured houses of **Primrose Hill**, which is the sort of place where rich rock stars buy homes – and into **Camden Town**, which is the sort of place future rock stars begin their careers.

● On Regent's Park Road the bus passes alongside **Cecil Sharp House**, home of the English Folk and Dance Society and a library of traditional music plundered by numerous folk singers and bands. Camden has had a rock 'n' roll swagger since the 1970s – the uniform is skinny jeans and leather jacket, the drink of choice lager. Look out for **The Dublin Castle** pub on the left at 94 Parkway (where Madness used to hang out in the 1980s, and where Blur and the Arctic Monkeys have plugged in their amps). Further down is **The Good Mixer**, epicentre of the mid-1990s Britpop scene. As you cross Camden High Street, look to the left for the **Electric Ballroom**, which opened in 1978; it's where bands such as Joy Division, The Smiths and Public Enemy have been recorded on countless bootleg tapes. As the 274 goes down Agar Grove and crosses Murray Street, you're within a few yards of **Camden Square**, where Amy Winehouse died at number 30 in 2011. Get off the bus at the **Angel Islington/City Road** terminus.

● Walk back to the City Road/Upper Street junction and turn right. Cross at the traffic lights outside Angel tube and turn right, then catch the northbound **4, 19, 30** or **43** from the **Angel Station** bus stop. Take this all the way up Upper Street to the stop opposite **Islington Town Hall** – where Paul McCartney and Linda Eastman got hitched, as well as Liam Gallagher and Patsy Kensit – then continue walking up Upper Street for a celebratory pint in **The Hope & Anchor** (on the left). This Victorian-era boozer lays claim to being the most famous rock pub in the country: its live shows helped coin the phrase 'pub rock' in the early 1970s, when bands such as Ian Dury's Kilburn and the High Roads played; later bills featured virtually every punk, ska and new-wave act you could name. You can see the pub in its heyday in the video to *One Step Beyond* by Madness. It's a lot smarter than it was then, but bands still play in the upstairs room – come here in the evening and you might be lucky enough to see the rock stars of the future

To download this journey to your Smartphone, scan the QR code (right).

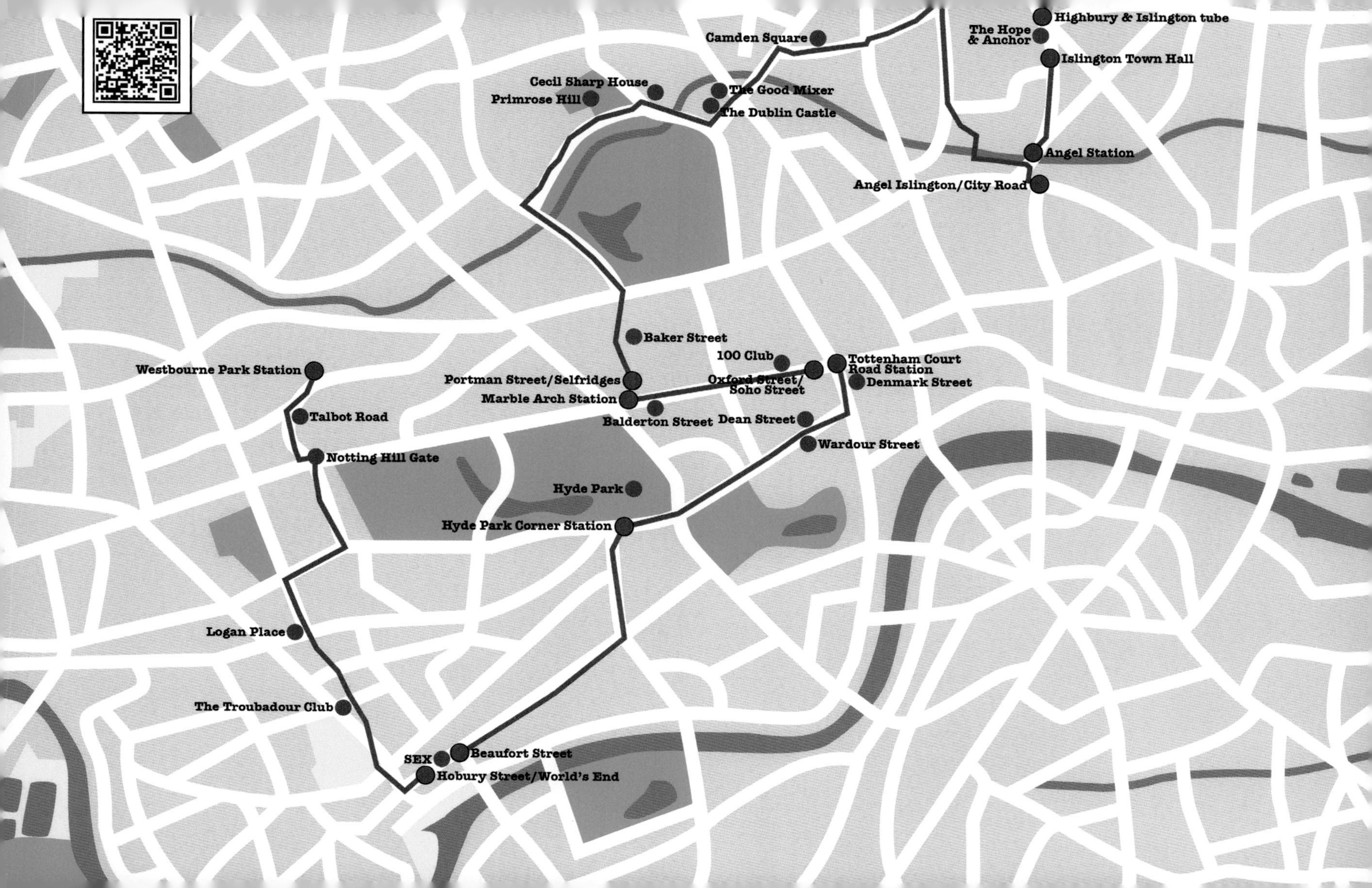
Camden Square
Highbury & Islington tube
The Hope
& Anchor
Islington Town Hall
Cecil Sharp House
Primrose Hill
The Good Mixer
The Dublin Castle
Angel Station
Angel Islington/City Road
Baker Street
100 Club
Tottenham Court
Road Station
Westbourne Park Station
Portman Street/Selfridges
Oxford Street/
Soho Street
Denmark Street
Marble Arch Station
Talbot Road
Balderton Street
Dean Street
Wardour Street
Notting Hill Gate
Hyde Park
Hyde Park Corner Station
Logan Place
The Troubadour Club
SEX
Beaufort Street
Hobury Street/World's End

23. sunday markets

Confirming its reputation as the city that never rests – even on the Sabbath – London hosts several busy markets every Sunday. Fabulously unfunctional, these wildly varied collections of stalls have never really existed to keep the city's wheels of commerce turning; the Sunday markets are much more about life's little luxuries – the non-essential goods that make shopping such an enjoyable and fun experience. So whether you're after fresh flowers in Hoxton, cutting-edge fashion at Brick Lane or original art in Greenwich – or simply some freshly cooked street food to accompany a lazy-afternoon pint with your friends – this journey will serve you well. Remember to take cash – and a large shopping bag.

Start point: Hoxton overground
End point: Cutty Sark DLR
Duration: 4 hours

● To make the most of London's Sunday markets, it's worth making an early start – try to get to **Hoxton overground** station by 9.30am. Once there, come out of either of the station exits and walk the few metres down to Cremer Street. Turn left here, then right down Hackney Road. After a few minutes, turn left into **Columbia Road** and walk along until you see the beginnings of the famous flower market. It was Huguenot weavers who introduced a taste for fresh flowers into the East End and several markets in this part of London began to supply this demand from the 16th century onwards. Columbia Road got its first stalls in 1869, when philanthropist Angela Burdett-Coutts decided to redevelop what had become one of the city's most notorious and dangerous slums. As the area around Hoxton and Spitalfields had a predominantly Jewish population at that time, special dispensation was given to allow Sunday trading. Nowadays stalls are piled high with everything from cut flowers to bedding plants, and the surrounding streets are filled with people struggling to carry trees and ornamental shrubs to the nearest tube stations. This regular Sunday-morning influx has attracted several stylish shops and cafés to the road and, like so many of the capital's best markets, Columbia Road has become a favourite weekend hangout for early rising Londoners.

● Once you've explored the market, retrace your steps to Hackney Road. Before you reach it, though, turn left down Virginia Road. Follow this road around the corner and turn left down Swanfield Street. When you reach the bottom, turn left along Bethnal Green Road, then right into **Brick Lane**. This street is well known for being the heart of Bangladeshi London, but on Sundays it gives itself over to a street market that is one of London's most idiosyncratic. You'll find all the East London staples – Cockney apple-sellers, Indian saris and jewellery, student-run juice bars – here, but it's the market's sheer unpredictability that makes it special. Nobody really knows what the stalls will be hawking from week to week, and there are always fantastic bargains to be had – especially for those with an eye for fashion and interiors. The Upmarket, in The Old Truman Brewery around halfway down the street, offers more than 140 stalls that specialise mainly in food or fashion. Check out the one run by Studio Ochee (www.studioochee.com) – designer of this book's cover illustration – which

Apple Market, Covent Garden

sells stunning, ethically made clothing you won't find anywhere else.

● Turn right onto Hanbury Street – immediately passing the spot on the right (now covered by a large modern building) where Jack the Ripper's second victim Annie Chapman was discovered in 1888 – and walk straight ahead until it meets Commercial Street. Cross the road and bear left into **Old Spitalfields Market**. This Victorian market hall may have been gentrified and spruced up in recent years – note the number of gleaming permanent shops and restaurants now incorporated into the structure – but it's still an East End raggle-taggle of pitches at heart. It's an excellent place in which to pick up budget fashion, art and homeware. And though the occasional piece of tourist tat makes an appearance, the market is close enough to east London's design schools to ensure a steady stream of innovative stallholders.

● Exit Old Spitalfields Market onto Brushfield Street (to the left of the point at which you entered) and turn right. When you reach Bishopsgate, cross the road, turn right then left into Primrose Street. At the end of this road, turn left into Appold Street and follow the road around the corner – at which point it becomes Sun Street – until you emerge in Finsbury Square. Walk straight ahead, then cross City Road and turn left to reach the **Finsbury Square** bus stop. Catch the northbound **214** from here.

● Get off the bus at the **Camden Town Station** stop and continue walking along Camden High Street, passing the tube station on your right. Though it's open all week, **Camden Market** is particularly busy on a Sunday. Ignore the touristy shops along Camden High Street and don't bother with the tacky enclosed section to the right – which, thanks to it being signposted 'Camden Market', has sucked in many a naïve visitor who's left without seeing the real thing. Carry on walking until you've crossed the canal and turn left into the market just before the railway bridge. From here, you're on your own. The warren-like lanes and paths through this sprawling and expansive market are almost unnavigable, so simply lose yourself for an hour or two amid stalls selling everything from vintage clothing and antique furniture to rare vinyl and rubber fetish gear.

● Head back towards Camden Town tube then, once you've passed it, turn left onto Camden Road (the one with The World's End pub on the corner). Catch the southbound **24** or **29** from the

Greenwich Market

Camden Town Station stop on the right-hand side and take the bus all the way down to **Leicester Square Station**.

● Continue walking down Charing Cross Road from the bus stop, then turn left into Cranbourn Street. At the crossroads, head along Garrick Street and turn left into King Street. Follow this road into **Covent Garden Market**. Though the market hall ahead of you hasn't dealt in flowers, fruit and vegetables since 1974 – when traders moved their operations to New Covent Garden Market in Battersea – it still retains a little of its original independent spirit amid the upmarket shops that now dominate. Several stalls, specialising in jewellery, arts and crafts, operate from the Apple Market in the front section of the main marketplace; and the Jubilee Market Hall, to the right of the piazza, provides a scuzzy contrast to the elegance across the square. If you've ever wondered where tourists bought their Union Jack top hats, you'll find the answer here.

● Walk to the back of the piazza (the end at which the Royal Opera House is situated) and head along Russell Street. Turn left up Bow Street then right along Long Acre; then, at the end of the road, head straight along Great Queen Street. When you reach Kingsway, cross over and turn right. Catch the southbound **188** from the **Holborn Station** stop.

● It's a long journey over Waterloo Bridge, and through Bermondsey and Rotherhithe, to the **Greenwich Town Centre/Cutty Sark** stop, so you'll no doubt be feeling hungry by the time you arrive. It's just as well, then, that **Greenwich Market** – the entrance to which can be seen from the bus stop – has a wonderful selection of street-food stalls at the northern end of its covered marketplace. As well as all the delicious, aromatic steam coming from that section, the pitches dedicated to fashion, accessories, art and crafts are colourful enough to send you into sensory overdrive. With a genteel air appropriate to this refined section of southeast London, the market is a lovely place to end up on a Sunday afternoon. Especially when there are pubs as good as the Greenwich Union and the Richard I just a few minutes walk away on Royal Hill.

● When you're ready to leave, simply retrace your footsteps to the **Greenwich Town Centre/Cutty Sark** bus stop and turn right off Creek Road to get to **Cutty Sark DLR**.

To download this journey to your Smartphone, scan the QR code (right).

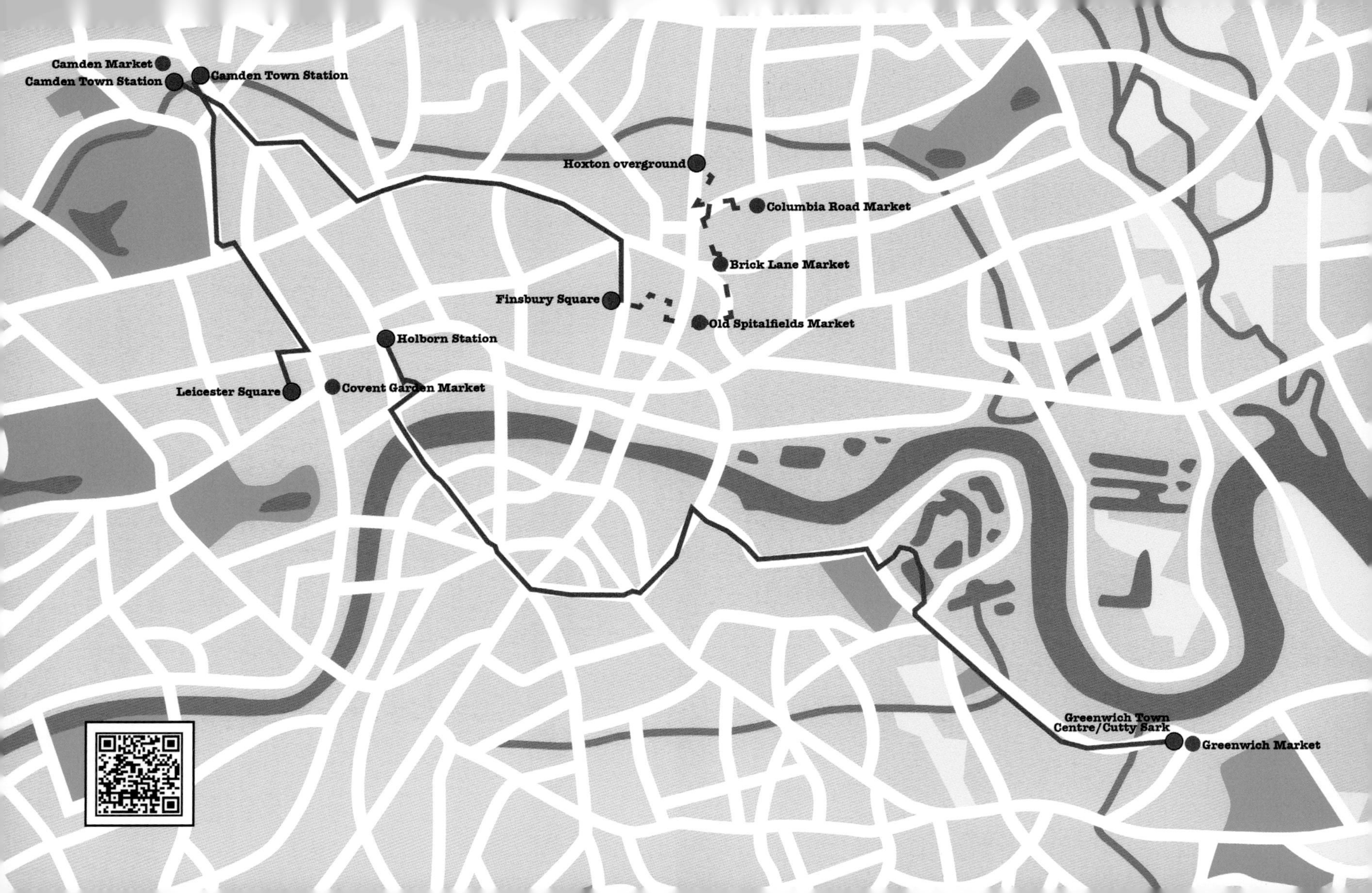
Camden Market
Camden Town Station
Camden Town Station
Hoxton overground
Columbia Road Market
Brick Lane Market
Finsbury Square
Old Spitalfields Market
Holborn Station
Leicester Square
Covent Garden Market
Greenwich Town Centre/Cutty Sark
Greenwich Market

Abney Park Cemetery, Stoke Newington

24. the victorian city

A glorious age in many ways, the reign of Queen Victoria from 1837 to 1901 saw unprecedented advances in science, technology and the arts. And London, as the centre of the British Empire, grew wealthy on the back of these. Fabulously ornate buildings went up as the capital redrew itself as the ultimate modern city, and gained its first underground railways, electric lights and a public-health system that brought an end to the epidemics that carried off huge swathes of the population. Things weren't all rosy, though. Behind the wealth and progress lay a parallel city – one of filthy slums and grinding poverty, from which the only escape was the workhouse. And, in Whitechapel, a serial murderer labelled Jack the Ripper began his killing spree, bringing the horror of the East End's medieval living conditions into the newly formed modern consciousness.

Start point: Farringdon tube
End point: Holborn tube
Duration: 5 hours

● If you've arrived at **Farringdon tube** via the line from King's Cross St Pancras, you've just experienced your first piece of London Victoriana. The city's first underground train line – the Metropolitan Railway – was opened in January 1863, and ran from Paddington Bishop's Road (now Paddington tube) to Farringdon Street, which is the station you've just disembarked at. Despite the fears of some clergy who worried that tunnelling underground might accidentally break through to Hell and unleash the Devil on the capital, work on the line was begun in 1860. The tunnels built then are still in daily use more than 150 years later.

● Come out of Farringdon tube and turn left down Cowcross Street. Walk right to the end and you'll emerge opposite **Smithfield Market**, housed in a glorious cast-iron structure designed by Sir Horace Jones in 1868. Turn right along Charterhouse Street and, at the end, turn left onto Farringdon Road. Cross the road and catch the northbound **45** from the **Snow Hill** bus stop.

● For London's greatest piece of Victorian Gothic Revival architecture, get off the bus at the **King's Cross Station/York Way** terminus and walk back down York Way. Turn right along Euston Road and you will be confronted with the soaring façade of **St Pancras Station**, Sir George Gilbert Scott's masterpiece. Built in 1865, it was earmarked for demolition in the 1960s but – mainly thanks to the efforts of poet John Betjeman – it survived, and now houses the upmarket St Pancras Renaissance Hotel as well as the national rail and Eurostar station. Its sheer beauty makes it the perfect symbol of Victorian authorities' aesthetic approach to public services.

● Continue along Euston Road and catch the northbound **476** from the **British Library** stop. After going through Islington and Newington Green, the bus heads down Stoke Newington Church Street. Look left here for a view of **Abney Park Cemetery**. As the capital's population was rapidly expanding in the 19th century and cremation was illegal until 1885, extra burial space was desperately required. This led to the creation of the 'magnificent seven' cemeteries – Abney Park, Brompton, Highgate, Kensal Green, Nunhead, Tower Hamlets and West Norwood – which were built around the fringes of central London between 1832 and 1841. Arboretum and graveyard were combined here at Abney Park, and today the cemetery is a wonderfully overgrown Victorian delight – filled with crumbling tombs and creepy angled headstones. You could happily idle away an entire day in here. Teenage Goths often do.

● Get off the bus at **Stoke Newington Station,** cross the road and turn left to catch the southbound **243** from the identically named stop on the other side. Get off the bus at the **Hoxton Station/ Geffrye Museum** stop and continue down Kingsland Road. Cross the road and turn right into Falkirk Street, then right up Hoxton Street. **Hoxton Hall,** a short walk up on the right, was built as MacDonald's Music Hall in 1863 to provide the local working-class community with a place in which they could indulge the Victorian appetite for revues of popular song, comedy and variety acts.

● Continue up Hoxton Street and you will see the unadulterated façade of the former **Shoreditch Workhouse**. Thanks to a law change in 1834, financial aid was withdrawn and the only option available to anyone unable to economically sustain themselves became the workhouse. The Victorian era saw thousands of unemployed workers and the elderly enter these institutions, where they were subjected to a daily routine of hard work and intense religious instruction that most were unable to escape from. The system was abolished in 1930 and many workhouses – Shoreditch included – became municipal hospitals instead.

● Immediately after passing the workhouse, turn right along Nuttall Street; then cross Kingsland Road and turn right to catch the southbound **242** from the **St Leonard's Hospital** stop. Once the bus passes St Leonard's Church on the church, it is travelling along the western boundary of the notorious **Old Nichol** slum – known as a rookery in Victorian parlance. Famous for its high levels of crime and destitution, Old Nichol was an overcrowded district of decaying, barely habitable houses with terrifyingly high rates of mortality. Slum clearance was a huge priority in the late Victorian era, and Old Nichol was demolished between 1891 and 1893 to be replaced by the current Boundary Estate. The bandstand you can glimpse at the end of Calvert Avenue, immediately on the left after St Leonard's Church, was built with rubble from the old slum houses.

● Get off the bus at **City Thameslink Station,** then cross the road and bear right to catch the eastbound **25** from the identically named stop on the other side. It immediately passes the Old Bailey, built

St Pancras Station

on the site of **Newgate Prison**, on the right. This is where the last public hanging in England – of Irish Fenian bomber Michael Barrett – took place in front of the prison walls. The execution was watched by a crowd of more than 2,000.

● Get off the bus at the **St Katherine Cree** stop, continue along Leadenhall Street and Aldgate, then turn left up Mitre Street. It was in **Mitre Square** – the entrance to which is on the right about halfway up here – that the mutilated body of Catherine Eddowes, the penultimate victim of Victorian serial killer Jack the Ripper, was found in November 1888. A potent symbol of late-Victorian London – who laid bare the horror behind the gilded facade of one of the world's wealthiest cities – Jack the Ripper forced upper- and middle-class Londoners to address the city's rookeries; districts in their midst where crime and prostitution were a way of life.

● Retrace your steps to Aldgate, cross the road and turn left. Catch the westbound **15** from the **Aldgate Station** stop and take the bus through the City and along Fleet Street. Once it enters the Strand, look to the left for the entrance to **The Savoy Theatre and Hotel**. Opened in 1881, the theatre was commissioned by impresario Richard D'Oyly Carte to stage the comic operas of WS Gilbert and Arthur Sullivan – *The Mikado* and *The Gondoliers* were among the productions to be premiered here. The theatre was the first public building in the world to be lit by electricity.

● Get off the bus at the **Charing Cross Station** stop, walk back and turn right down Villiers Street. Walk straight through Embankment tube and cross the road. Turn right along the **Victoria Embankment** and walk past the monuments to WS Gilbert and pioneering civil engineer Joseph Bazalgette. Despite not being particularly well-known these days, Bazalgette's contribution to Victorian London is arguably the greatest of all. It was the revolutionary sewer system he designed and implemented for the capital between 1865 and 1875 that brought an end to the cholera epidemics that had claimed the lives of more than 20,000 Londoners over the previous 50 years. Bazalgette's foresight meant that the 1,800 kilometres of sewer pipes he installed beneath the city streets were able to cope with London's population explosion in the 20th century, and are still in use today.

● Continue along the Victoria Embankment – another of Bazalgette's creations – until it meets Westminster Bridge. Cross Bridge Street and turn right to walk alongside Big

The Albert Memorial,
Kensington Gardens

Ben and the **Houses of Parliament.** This breathtaking display of Victorian Gothic Revival design was built between 1836 and 1870 under the direction of architects Charles Barry and Augustus Pugin. The pair were awarded the commission after the original Palace of Westminster burned down in 1834.

● Turn left and walk across the facade of the Houses of Parliament then, on the far side of Parliament Square, turn right and walk across the front of **Westminster Abbey** – where Queen Victoria was crowned in June 1838 – to the **Parliament Square/Westminster Abbey** bus stop. Take the westbound **148** from here all the way to **Queensway Station.** Just before the bus reaches Victoria Station, look left to see the Neo Byzantine **Westminster Cathedral,** which is the centre of English and Welsh Catholicism. It was built in 1885, just over 50 years after the Roman Catholic Church was officially restored to the country after an absence of more than three centuries.

● Walk back from the Queensway Station stop and enter Kensington Gardens through Black Lion Gate. Follow the Broad Walk path all the way through the park, passing the statue of Queen Victoria (sculptured by her daughter Princess Louise) outside **Kensington Palace** – where the Queen was born in 1819.

● When you emerge from the park, turn right and catch the eastbound **10** from the **Palace Gate** stop. Look left for Sir George Gilbert Scott's 1872 **Albert Memorial,** commissioned by Victoria to commemorate her beloved late husband. The bus heads along the southern edge of Hyde Park, which is where the Great Exhibition of 1851 – at which all the latest cultural and innovations were showcased – was held in the 92,000sq m Crystal Palace.

● Get off the bus at the **Tottenham Court Road Station** stop and continue along Oxford Street and New Oxford Street – the northern boundary of the notorious **St Giles** rookery (now demolished) – onto High Holborn. End your journey around Victorian London at **The Princess Louise** on the right. Not only is this pub named after Queen Victoria's sculptress daughter, but it is also one of the most authentic Victorian taverns in the capital. The tiled bar areas, frosted screens – designed to keep the social classes apart – and stucco ceiling are impressive enough, but wait until you visit the toilets. They're Grade-II listed

To download this journey to your Smartphone, scan the QR code (right).

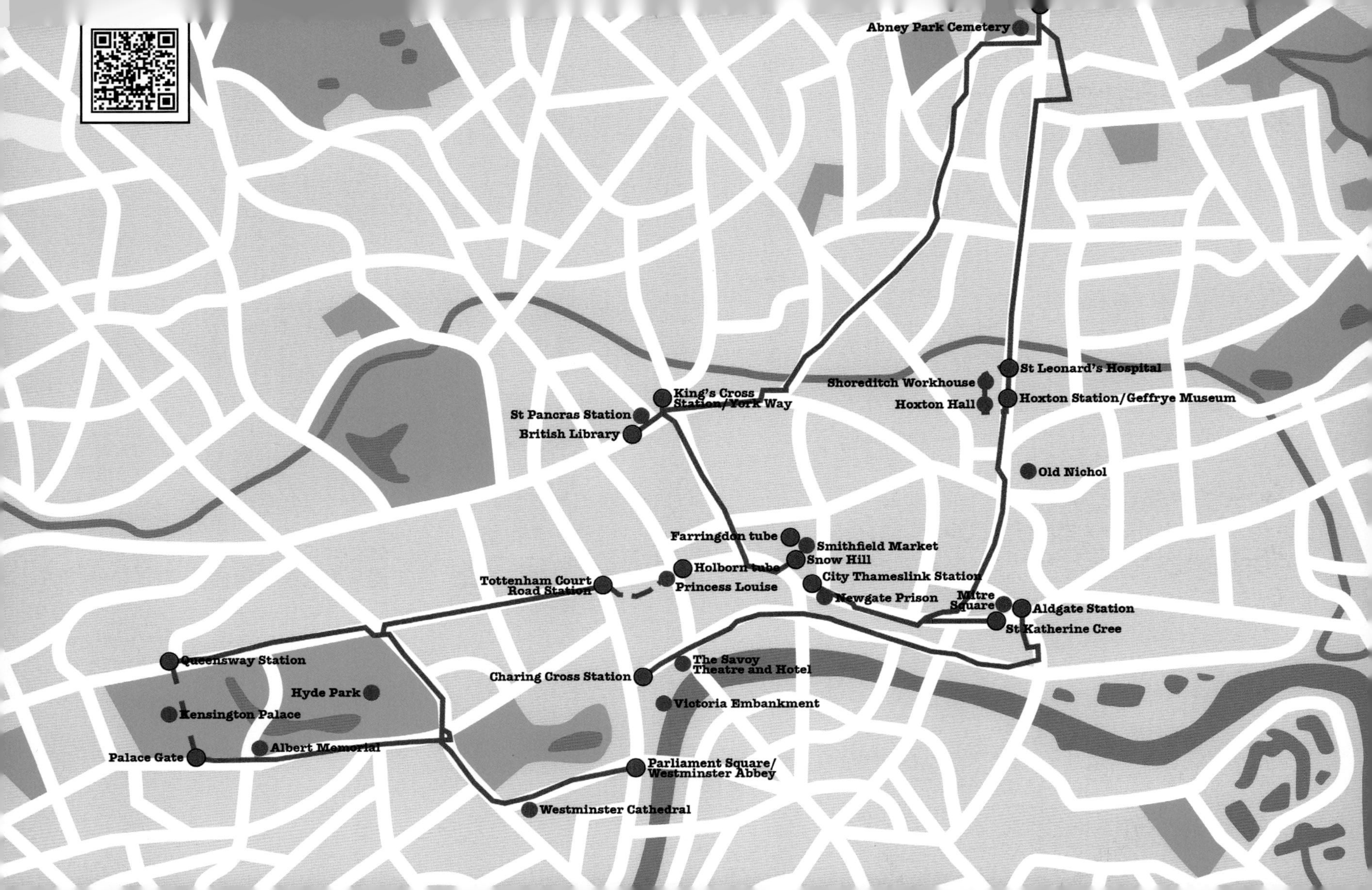
Abney Park Cemetery
St Leonard's Hospital
Shoreditch Workhouse
Hoxton Station/Geffrye Museum
Hoxton Hall
Old Nichol
King's Cross Station/York Way
St Pancras Station
British Library
Farringdon tube
Smithfield Market
Snow Hill
Holborn tube
City Thameslink Station
Tottenham Court Road Station
Princess Louise
Newgate Prison
Mitre Square
Aldgate Station
St Katherine Cree
Queensway Station
The Savoy Theatre and Hotel
Charing Cross Station
Hyde Park
Victoria Embankment
Kensington Palace
Albert Memorial
Palace Gate
Parliament Square/ Westminster Abbey
Westminster Cathedral

Statue of Paddington Bear at the station from which he takes his name

25. london for children

An exciting place in which to grow up, and even more fascinating to visit, London is as thrilling for kids as a bucketful of blue Smarties. Its thousands of child-friendly attractions – which include everything from lion-spotting at the zoo and button-pressing at the Science Museum to dedicated children's festivals and theatre performances – are well documented, but the city also boasts many free (and permanent) sites that are sure to fire the imagination of any wide-eyed infant. This bus journey takes in some of the famous places that no child will want to miss, as well as several more obscure – though no less enjoyable – landmarks. Adults, take note. There's no need to grow up and act your age on this trip.

Start point: South Kensington tube
End point: Bethnal Green tube
Duration: 4.5 hours

● Turn right after the ticket barriers at **South Kensington tube**, then walk along the tunnel that leads to the **Natural History Museum**. Admission is free, and you'll see your first dinosaur skeleton – a 26-metre-long diplodocus – as soon as you go through the museum's main entrance. The Dinosaurs area, which features an animatronic tyrannosaurus rex among all the bones and teeth, is located immediately to the left of here.

● Though wonderful, the Natural History Museum is huge enough to exhaust even the most enthusiastic six-year-old. So, as soon as you've seen the dinosaurs, leave through the main entrance. Turn left outside the museum gates and walk for a couple of minutes (crossing Exhibition Road) to catch the eastbound **14**, **74** or **414** from the **Victoria & Albert Museum** bus stop. Get off at the **Hyde Park Corner Station** stop.

● There are several bus stops with the same name along this stretch of road, so locate the one from which the eastbound **9** departs. Take this bus all the way to the **Southampton Street** stop, continue walking along the Strand then turn left up Southampton Street. **Covent Garden**, at the top of the road, is home to the sort of places – Benjamin Pollock's Toyshop, The London Transport Museum, Eric Snook's fun store – that will have children asking for their pocket money. It is also famed for its street performers, and many a parent has tarried here with a coffee for half an hour while their offspring gawp at magicians, acrobats and statue-still art students dressed as Charlie Chaplin.

● Walk the short distance back to the Strand by heading along Henrietta Street, which runs along the left-hand side of St Paul's Church at the front of the piazza, then turning left down Bedford Street. At the bottom, cross the road and catch the westbound **6** or **23** from the **Bedford Street** stop directly opposite. Both these buses pass **Hamleys Toy Store** on the right as they make their way up Regent Street. This seven-storey, 5,000sq m temple to toys – the biggest store of its kind in the world – will be the highlight of any child's day if you take them here.

● Get off the bus at the **Marble Arch Station** stop, then catch the westbound **94** or **390** from the identically named stop a little further along the road. Both buses take you along the perimeter of

The Elfin Oak,
Kensington Gardens

Hyde Park and Kensington Gardens. Look out for the house on the corner of Leinster Terrace and Bayswater Road (marked by a blue plaque), which is where author JM Barrie wrote *Peter and Wendy* – the story that introduced Peter Pan, Captain Hook and Tinkerbell to the world.

● Get off the bus at **Queensway Station,** then walk back and enter Kensington Gardens through Black Lion Gate. Walk down the path straight ahead and bear right when you reach the café. To one side of this stands the **Elfin Oak**, a tree stump that swarms with wooden elves, fairies and miniature animals, which was created by artist Ivor Innes in the late 1920s. Behind the oak is the entrance to the **Diana Memorial Playground,** a huge play space that opened in 2000 as a memorial to the late princess. Inspired by Barrie's Peter Pan story, the enormous playground contains a recreation of a pirate ship, as well as tipis, a beach and climbing apparatus.

● When the kids have had enough of this mock Neverland, leave the park through Black Lion Gate, then cross the road and turn right. Catch the eastbound **94, 148** or **390** from the **Queensway Station** bus stop. Take a short ride to **Lancaster Gate Station,** then get off the bus and continue walking up Lancaster Terrace. Bear left around Sussex Gardens and carry straight on up Westbourne Terrace, then turn right into Craven Road. The entrance to **Paddington Station** is on the left just after a hotel. Once you're on the station concourse, turn left and walk into the piazza area directly behind platforms 3 and 4. Here you'll find Marcus Cornish's sculpture of Paddington Bear – the famous 1950s children's character who, in Michael Bond's story, was found at this station.

● Retrace your steps to Craven Road, then turn left down Praed Street. Catch the eastbound **205** from the **Paddington Station** stop, get off at **King's Cross Station** and walk onto the station concourse. Bear left towards platforms 9, 10 and 11, located in a separate building, and you will see **Platform 9 ¾** on the right. As any Harry Potter fan will tell you, this is the departure point for the Hogwarts Express – the train that takes young witches and wizards to Hogwarts School of Witchcraft and Wizardry in JK Rowling's books and the subsequent films. A luggage trolley disappearing into the brickwork hints at a magical platform on the other side of the wall.

● Return to the **King's Cross Station** stop and catch the southbound **45** or **46** from the identically named stop a couple of

Coram's Fields

metres to the right. Get off the bus at the **Guilford Street** stop, continue walking down Gray's Inn Road and turn right into Guilford Street. Walk along the road for a few minutes and you will arrive at the entrance gates to **Coram's Fields** – a 28,000sq m park dedicated to children. Adults must be accompanying a child to enter Coram's Fields and the space – which includes a nursery, children's centre, café, on-site farm and well-maintained play areas – is a safe and peaceful haven for kids and parents. The park is laid out on the former site of London's 18th-century Foundling Hospital, which is where many a deserted or orphaned child found sanctuary from the 1700s until as late as the 1920s.

● When you leave Coram's Fields, turn right onto Guilford Street and continue walking in a straight line until you reach Russell Square. Cross over the road, turn left and walk around the bottom of the square until you emerge at the top of Montague Street. Walk down here then turn right onto Great Russell Street. You will find yourself at the entrance to the **British Museum**. As at the Natural History Museum, there is so much to see in here that children can easily be overwhelmed. If you do go in (admission is free), head straight for the Egyptian mummies in Rooms 62 and 63 on level three. Children will find these a lot more exciting than the Elgin Marbles, we promise you...

● When you emerge from the British Museum, bear right across the zebra crossing outside the main gates and walk straight down Museum Street. At the bottom of the road, turn left up Bloomsbury Way and catch the eastbound **55** from the **Museum Street** bus stop. Get off at the **Cambridge Heath Station** stop, continue along Hackney Road, then turn right down Cambridge Heath Road. Walk on for five minutes or so, and you will find yourself at the **V&A Museum of Childhood**. This gorgeous 19th-century building houses the Victoria & Albert Museum's fascinating collection of toys, games and child-related artefacts, and features playthings that date from the 1600s to the present day. Admission is free and parents will be glad to hear the museum also offers a café to offset all that excitable squealing over Dinky cars and 1980s He-Man figures.

● Once you've finished at the museum, simply turn left outside the gates and walk down to **Bethnal Green tube**.

To download this journey to your Smartphone, scan the QR code (right).

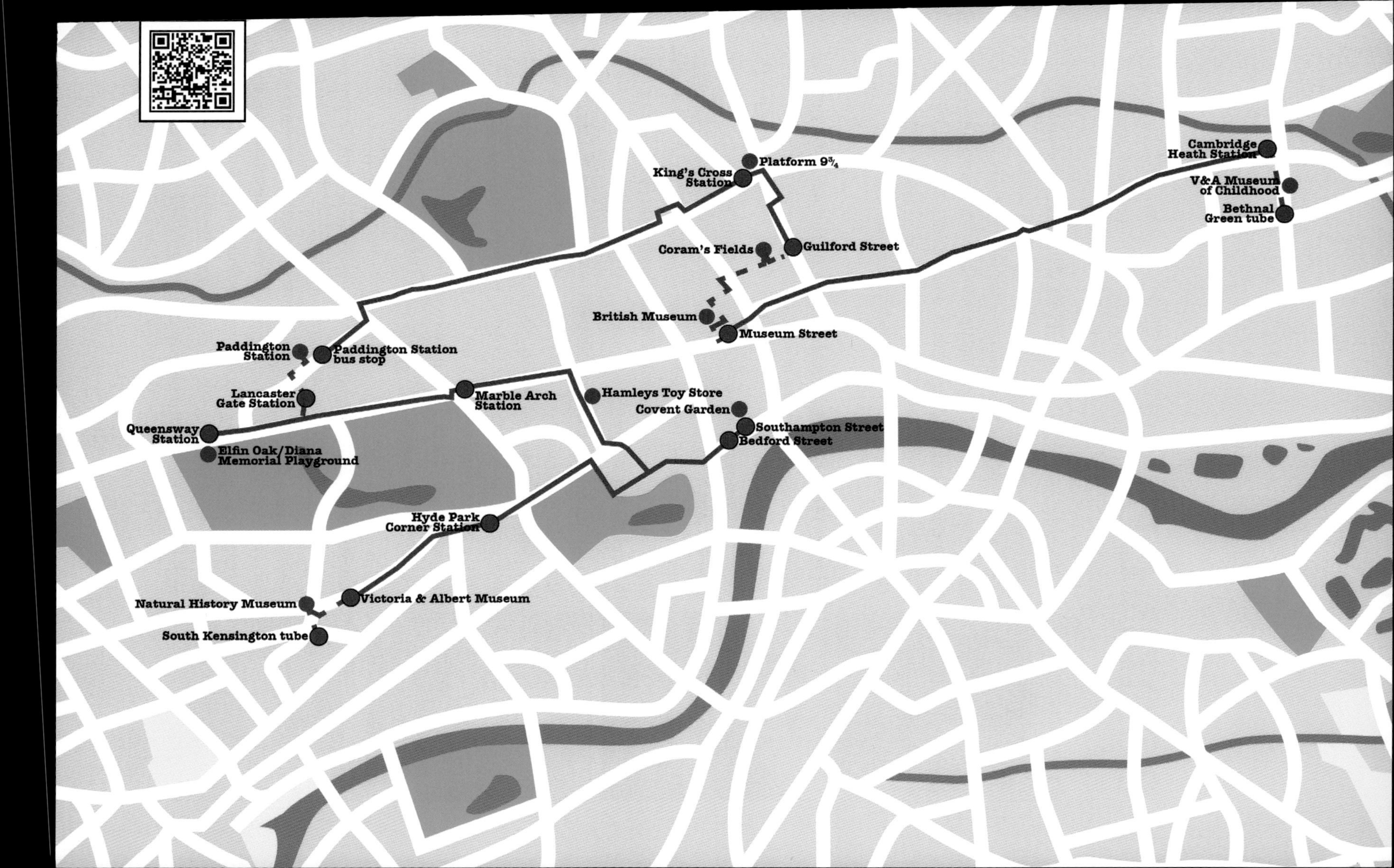

Cambridge Heath Station
V&A Museum of Childhood
Bethnal Green tube
Platform 9¾
King's Cross Station
Coram's Fields
Guilford Street
British Museum
Museum Street
Paddington Station
Paddington Station bus stop
Lancaster Gate Station
Marble Arch Station
Hamleys Toy Store
Covent Garden
Southampton Street
Bedford Street
Queensway Station
Elfin Oak/Diana Memorial Playground
Hyde Park Corner Station
Natural History Museum
Victoria & Albert Museum
South Kensington tube

contributors

Self-confessed music addict **Rick Jordan**, author of 'London's musical landmarks', lives in north London and travels the world – mainly vicariously – for *Condé Nast Traveller* magazine. To make a portable jukebox for your journey, he suggests you load your iPod with *London Calling* by The Clash; *Folk, Blues and Beyond* by Davey Graham; and *Under Milk Wood* by British jazz pianist Stan Tracey.

Ginny Henry, writer of 'Followers of fashion', worked as a stylist before gravitating to the world of women's magazines, where she works as a Picture Editor. With a sideline in jewellery design, she doesn't have much time to explore her adopted home city, but when she gets a moment, can usually be found in the costume and jewellery galleries at the V&A, or in Liberty; taking inspiration from the former and bankrupting herself in the latter.

Though journalist **Philip Clough** – who wrote the 'Ancient London' and 'Medieval & Tudor London' chapters – has spent the past 15 years exploring the highways, byways and oddities of London, he is a country boy at heart. Originally from Lancashire's Ribble Valley, he is a keen hill walker with a particular penchant for the Lake District, and a regular contributor to *Country Walking* and *Lakeland Walker* magazines.

Lawrence Potter, who wrote 'Babylon by bus', is the author of two books – *Mathematics Minus Fear* and *This May Help You Understand The World*, a collection of accessible essays on current international issues. If you ever wanted to know the difference between a Sunni and a Shia or how the US electoral process works, this is the book for you. He lives in south London with his beautiful wife Nancy and their bald son Frank.

index

available shortly

PARIS BY BUS
25 HIP HOPS AROUND THE FRENCH CAPITAL ON A BUDGET
RUFUS PURDY

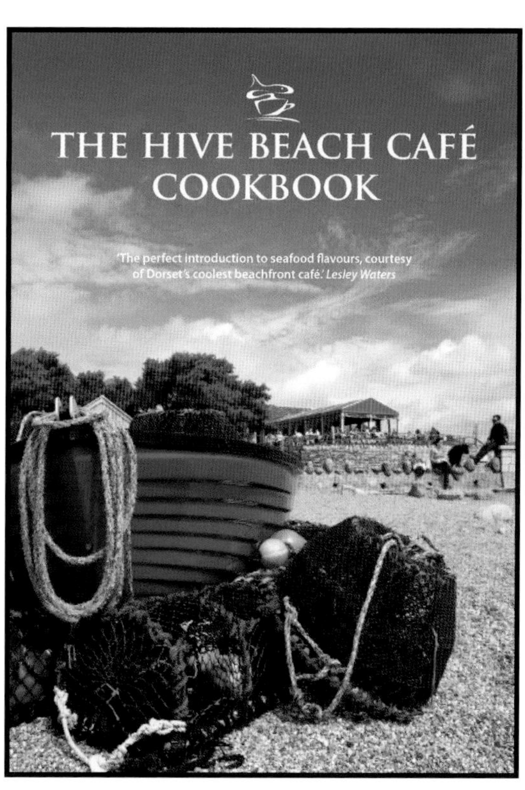
THE HIVE BEACH CAFÉ COOKBOOK
'The perfect introduction to seafood flavours, courtesy of Dorset's coolest beachfront café.' Lesley Waters

thank you

Rufus Purdy and **Bristlebird Books** would like to thank all the people that made this book possible. You know who you are – but not everyone else does, so here goes...

Firstly, a huge thank you to the *London By Bus* contributors **Philip Clough**, **Rick Jordan** and **Lawrence Potter**, who gave up their free time to road-test and write four of the themed bus journeys included in this book. **Nancy Potter**, who took several of the photographs, was also beyond brilliant. It's not easy to line up shots with a three-month-old baby strapped to your chest, but she managed it... **Ginny Henry**, as always, was an unbelievable help. As well as writing the 'Fashion trips' bus journey, she also turned her picture-editing genius to the images that appear throughout the book. Thank you all.

We'd also like to thank **Sarah Maber** for her excellent ideas, never-erring good sense and constant support of this project. And without the help of **Alice Purdy** and **Jasmina Isic**, it's unlikely this book would have happened at all. We appreciate your efforts more than we can possibly say.

Finally, a huge thank you to **Guy Staniforth**, without whom there would be no Bristlebird Books and certainly no *London By Bus*. You're an absolute star. Even if you are a Sheffield United fan.

www.bristlebird.co.uk